Don't Talk to the DUNNYMAN

JAMES PALMER

BALBOA
PRESS
A DIVISION OF HAY HOUSE

Balboa Press books may be ordered through booksellers or by contacting:

Balboa Press
A Division of Hay House
1663 Liberty Drive
Bloomington, IN 47403
www.balboapress.com.au
1 (877) 407-4847

Print information available on the last page.

ISBN: 978-1-5043-1441-1 (sc)
ISBN: 978-1-5043-1440-4 (e)

Balboa Press rev. date: 08/29/2018

This book was written with a lot of help, a huge thank you to my dear cousins, without their hours of work and endless encouragement I know this book would not have been, love you both.

Also thanks to their good friend who did some of the delightful pencil drawings in this book and was such a pleasure for them to work with.

To my wife especially and my sons who wanted to know more about what things were like back then.

This is inspired by actual events or a true story

In life if we are fortunate we make lots of friends if we are more then fortunate we also have a couple of mates and I dedicate this book to one of mine Wiffo who sadly isn't here to share this finished book with me.

CHAPTER ONE

"I'LL BE YOUR BROTHER AN' YOU CAN BE ME MATE"

"Wotcha doin'?" a voice from around the side of the house asked.

The startled reply came quickly, "Just takin' the stuff out of the car an' into the house." The boy replying to the question was trying desperately to locate the face behind the original voice.

"Are ya gonna live in this house?" the hidden voice asked.

"Reckon so," still striving to put a face to the voice.

At this, a figure materialised from the shadow of the dunny. 'That means that your old man must be the new boss man at the council.' At last the person behind the voice appeared, he was a young aboriginal boy about ten years old, and it was little wonder his whereabouts had been hard to pinpoint as he was as black as the inside of your hat.

"Me name's Cedric but they call me Ceddy," he said revealing the most amazing white teeth you would ever see, "Are ya allowed t' talk to me?"

"You're here, so 'course I can," came the answer although a little puzzled by the question, "I'm John an' we just got here ya know."

"Yep! I seen ya drive in, Kondie reckoned that ya wouldn't be here for another week or so, 'cause of the wet."

"Well Londie was nearly right; we come through a lot of stuff to get here, an' why were ya hiding behind the dunny?"

"I weren't hidin' I was just comin' from my place, an' his name is Kondie. I reckon you mob will be the first through since the wet started, even the train didn't run for a couple of weeks."

The wet, as it is affectionately called, had blanketed the entire state and, at this time of the year, movement by car, especially in this part of outback Queensland, was almost zero. John's parents had considered the problems that would be involved in their family traveling over this period, however the decision to 'plug on regardless' had worked in the past, so why not this time?

The three brothers always dreaded it when their father asked at the dinner table, "How would you like to live in, *such and such?*" This statement invariably meant that the family would soon be on the move again.

Arthur' profession as a surveyor meant that finding work was usually not a problem, which was probably a good thing as he didn't always deal well with authority, especially if they were not as competent as he felt they should have been.

Arthur and his wife Isobel together with their three sons Charles, John and Edward had lived from Gordenvale to Griffith up to New Guinea and a lot of stops in between. In general, the boys took their nomadic life style in their stride, and from past experience they knew the trip itself would not be without adventure.

With the wet already started they were sure this one would be no different to any of the other nine or ten times they had moved. This relocation, however, held a lot of promise for the boys, as the prospect of living in a town other than the current one, and going to a school other than their current one, sounded too good to be true.

They knew that the journey of over two thousand miles would be by far the longest single move they had undertaken, but the thought of seeing the last of Ballon put everything else aside.

Maybe if they had been able to foresee what lay in store for them during the trip, a few weeks delay might have been sensible. Cramped together in an Austin A30 Countryman, the family had battled the elements since leaving the southern Queensland border town four weeks earlier. On occasions food had been short and dry clothes were worn only when in the car. This poor little vehicle had been pushed, towed and dug out of creeks, rivers and bogs, along almost the entire length of the state. Days had been spent camped on the banks of creeks or rivers waiting for the waters to subside only to find another one over the road a few miles further on.

The mighty Burdekin River had been crossed on a flat bed rail car with the raging flood water lapping at the underside of the bridge. Although probably illegal, for the family to get to the other side they had travelled across the ancient wooden structure crammed together inside their vehicle. With hardly walking room to the edge of the railway flatbed the boys could see the flood debris building up against the underside of the bridge and could feel the entire construction moving with the force of the water.

While the male members of the family may have been concerned with the mass of water, the crossing must have been absolutely terrifying for the boy's mother, Isobel who, unlike the males in the family, could not swim a stroke. Years later while driving over the new high level concrete and steel structure she confessed that making that crossing was the most terrifying thing she had done in her life.

Probably aware of his wife's fear of water, once the nerve-racking crossing was complete and they were back on the road, Arthur remarked to his wife, "Well, that is definitely the worst of it behind us."

Two weeks later and only five hundred miles to show for it he had turned to her again and said, "Mmmm Isobel, this must be the place that the bloke at the pub said there would be a bit of water on the road."

"A bit!" she had exploded, "That looks like the bloody English Channel!"

'No.' Arthur replied quite seriously, 'The English Channel is twenty six miles across, whereas the bloke in the pub said this expanse of water only goes for about eight miles. Hence the name 'the eight mile swamp'."

Isobel was obviously not happy but rather then continuing the conversation she got out of the car and started to gather wood to make a fire. For their part the boys knew enough to keep their heads down, and help with any tasks they could so as not to provoke their mother.

Half an hour later things had cooled somewhat, the billy was on and the options for completing the final forty or so miles of their journey were being discussed.

Now, don't think for one minute that the three brothers had a lot of input into these meetings but as was the family tradition they were at least included and at times their parents listened to what they had to say.

"If this is a swamp, then it could take a long time for the water to go down enough for us to drive through." said Isobel as she expertly rolled a cigarette.

"That's right," nodded her husband in agreement. "But the publican was telling me that most people put their vehicles on the railway track as it is built up above the water level."

"That will work OK, if we can get the car across the damn table drain and up onto the tracks." came the heated reply.

At this point the entire meeting moved to the side of the road and the family surveyed the fifty, or so, feet of drain and slope that separated the road from the railway tracks.

"John," said Arthur to his middle son. "Walk into the drain and tell me what the bottom is like, will you?"

Only too happy to be asked to help, the boy, barefoot as usual, splashed into the slushy ankle deep water. He scratched at the bottom and walked across to where the water and the slope of the rail tracks met.

"The mud is slippery but the bottom is quite hard, an' as you can see, it's not very deep."

"Ah! That's good. This means we can use some gravel from the railway plus a few logs and build a little corduroy. By doing that we will cut down some of the slope up to the rails and keep us out of the slippery mud in the bottom of the drain."

As with most eternal optimists Arthur's ideas were wonderful as just that - 'ideas'. However, their application was nearly always a combination of the original plan plus a number of modifications, usually instigated by his much underestimated wife.

This type of undertaking was nothing new for the family and as they worked, Charles and John chatted away about what they expected in their new town.

"How big d' ya reckon it will be?" John asked his older brother.

"I don't know but I don't think it will be as big as Ballon."

"Gee, I hope it's better than that place. That was the most worst school I have ever been to."

Older by two years, but wiser by a lot more, Charles said, "Don't worry, this town will be a ripper and I know we'll be jake at the school."

As usual John accepted his older sibling's statement as gospel and worked even harder to complete the ramp across the drain and up to the railway line, almost as if suddenly he was looking forward to the prospect of a new town and school.

Three very wet, muddy and tiring hours later the little green Austin A30 was finally on the tracks and straddling one of the rails. The family's struggle to cross the drain and up the four feet slope had been hindered by the constant attacks from the air by nesting swamp plovers. These aggressive birds made life so uncomfortable that they took turns as the plover lookout.

Now that the car was actually in position to cross the swamp the worry that a train might come along became very real. Even though the publican had assured Arthur the rail motor was not due for another two days it was decided that John and Charles were to be dispatched on ahead to flag it down if the information given across the bar proved to be incorrect.

This suited the boys down to the ground as, for the first time since leaving Ballon almost four weeks earlier, they were able to get out of their parents' way, and as soon as they got far enough ahead they slipped out of their clobber and went for a quick dip in one of the numerous creeks that formed the eight mile swamp.

"Do ya reckon there are any crocs in here?" John asked his older brother, more interested than worried.

"We won't be in long enough for a croc t' get us, 'cause Mum an' Dad won't be far behind" was the reply.

"Too right! Mum's in a crook mood from getting the car on the tracks, don't wanna stir her up any more 'cause she'll spit the dummy for sure."

They swam for a few minutes more, then, reluctantly got out. It was then that they noticed that the car was not catching up and appeared to be stopped.

"Looks like she's stuck or broken down."

"Aw strewth I reckon ya right. Oh well, no good winging about it; we gotta go back an' help."

They arrived back at the car and quickly realised that the little A30 was having a few problems, the main one of these was the lack of clearance between the car sump and the railway line. This meant the weight in the car had to be kept to a minimum. Bar the driver, everyone including the youngest son, Edward, was walking.

Even with this precaution the crunch of metal on metal was heard a number of times especially where there was a little less gravel between the sleepers. There were also a number of small bridges like the one the two older boys had swum from and where the distance between the sleepers was such that the small wheels on the little Austin went down between them.

To solve this, sticks of a reasonable thickness were bound together with fishing line like a little mat about eight inches wide, these formed bridges between the sleepers and were moved continually from the rear to the front of the vehicle, this way only a half a dozen or so of the mats were required.

The reason the car wasn't moving when the boys had decided to return to it was that one of the first mats that had been made had broken and the wheel had gone right between the sleepers with the car finishing up with the sill panel almost on the sleeper. The adults were surveying the damage and working out what course of action would be required. The boys' return went unnoticed until John commented, "Gees we're in a bit of strife!" The statement got nothing but a deadly stare from both his parents.

In order to slide another mat under the suspended wheel the little car had to be jacked up; but the lack of any clearance between the car and the railway sleeper meant no room to get a jack under to lift it up. Eventually a sapling of considerable length was cut and the side of the car was levered up high enough to get the jack underneath in order to complete the job. Naturally when, a few minutes later, a second one snapped it was a lot less dramatic as they now knew just what was required having even kept the sapling they had used for a lever.

By now it was late afternoon and the physical effort over the past eight hours was starting to take its toll on children and adults alike, also because no one knew exactly how far they had to travel on the rail lines the concern that they may not reach the northern side of the swamp before dark was getting greater and greater with every turn of the little Austin's wheels.

Then just on dusk, reach it they did, and to their delight and great relief, getting off the tracks and back onto the road was easy. As luck would have it just where the swamp finished the road turned across the railway tracks this meant they literally drove straight back onto it.

Even though everyone would have loved a cuppa, Arthur opted not to put the billy on again and to push on to their destination. Two hours later at about nine o'clock, tired and cranky yet not without some satisfaction and using the road map of the town sent to them in the mail, they had pulled into the back yard of what was to be their new home.

"Some stuff of yours come on the rail motor last week." John's new companion informed him, "Kondie put it on the front verandah for ya."

This was good news especially in light of the fact that the little A30 had only been able to carry the family and the bare essentials for the trip.

Ceddy followed as John went to tell his parents what he had just learned.

"This is Ceddy." he said making the introduction to his parents. "He knows the bloke that put our stuff on the verandah."

"Yep, that's Kondie me Uncle, he works on the council." As he spoke his eyes darted around the entire family as if to take in as much information as he could in as short a time as possible. "He told me to say if you was the new boss an' ya wanna hand to unload t' give 'im a shout."

"That is good of your Uncle, Ceddy." said Arthur "but I think we will be able to manage."

Picking up on the boy's obvious disappointment at the reply, Isobel interrupted saying, "You could give John a hand to unpack the car if you would like, er - if you don't have to go home that is."

Ceddy's face immediately lit up like a beacon, "bonza missus I'd love t' give ya a hand an' I don't have to be home for ages."

A little while later when the car was almost unloaded a man approached the house through the park at the back. Like John's newfound friend he was very black, but that is where the similarity stopped, as this man was huge. Probably over six foot six and weighing in excess of seventeen stone his size alone should have frightened the boys, yet, as with most gentle giants, his presence had a nice calming effect.

"G'day," he said to John in a soft husky voice that was certainly out of keeping with his immense frame, "Is Ceddy here, I told him to come and git me t' help ya t' unpack."

At this moment Ceddy and the adults appeared from inside the house, "The Mister and Missus said they would be OK, an' they said thanks for the offer, an' they said I cun help 'em with the unpackin'."

At this the big man smiled and, like his nephew, a message of welcome was given without even a word being spoken. "I'm Kondie," he said extending his hand, "I reckon you must be me new boss."

"Arthur Tiley," came the reply, allowing his hand to be engulfed in Kondie's huge paw, "Thanks for getting our stuff from the railway and for the offer to help."

At this his wife spoke, offering her hand as well, "I'm Isobel and this is Charles, John and Edward."

As many before him, he smiled at the boys' names but did not make the usual 'bit of royalty there eh?' comment, that always followed when they were introduced as a group.

The brothers in turn shook his hand and when it was John's turn he said, "Pleased t' meet ya Mr. Kondie."

He held the boy's hand a little longer than the others and looking him in the eye said, "I'm not a mister young fella. Ya just call me Kondie."

All eyes swung to their father who said, "Er sorry, the boys have to call all adults mister."

"Okay by me." said the big man, "But I reckon ya will find it a bit strange in this town for a white kid t' call a boong mister."

Here Isobel spoke again "What are you the most comfortable with?"

"I think the kids should just call me Kondie like everyone else in town." he said, but then quickly added. "I'm not under the Act ya know so I don't have t' live on the settlement."

"OK" came the reply, "Kondie it is."

This was not the first time the problem of whether to call someone Mister or not had arisen, however this was the first time that the boys' parents had agreed to let them call an adult by their first name.

John was surprised by this and made a mental note to take it up with his mother at a future time.

The house that the family were to live in was obviously new as there were still a lot of builder's bits and pieces lying around.

Kondie filled his new boss in on what was going on. "The painter 'as been on the booze for the last week an' the bloke who was doing the ceiling broke his arm in a blue at the pub last Saterdy."

"No worries." accompanied a nod, "She'll be right for the time being. At least the beds are in and the kitchen is up and running."

"I cut some wood and collected some chips" said Ceddy. "I can start the stove if ya want."

The middle one of the three sons was pleased to hear this as one of his pocket money jobs was to ensure that the wood box was always full and there were plenty of chips to get the stove started in the morning.

"Thanks." said his Mother "But we are only going to have a sandwich and a cup of tea tonight."

"When I seen ya arrive I reckoned that ya might want a bite an' a cuppa, so I asked Polly t' make up a billy a' tea an' bring some bully beef an' bread over. She wanted to make up the bread and bully into a sanga but I told her not to 'cause ya might not like someone else making food for ya." Again the boys let a comment that they didn't understand slip by and even though their Mother and Father obviously reacted to it they did not say anything that would require Kondie to expand on his statement.

"That is very thoughtful." said Isobel, "Can we walk to your place or will we drive?"

Kondie looked startled, "Ya can't come to my place. Polly 's bringin' the tucker over here."

A few minutes later Polly turned up with a loaf of bread, butter, a tin of bully beef and a billy of steaming hot tea. "G'day Mister, Missus, Kondie reckoned ya might like a bit a tucker," she said in a high pitched sing-song voice.

"Thanks a lot." said Isobel "We'll put it on the kitchen table and everyone can have a bite."

Polly, unlike the two men in her family was small and as thin as a rake and the white dress she wore hung on her as if it was on a coat hanger. It was obvious that speaking understandable English did not come easily. She seemed very shy and had to be asked twice before coming into the house, even then she refused to sit down at the table with the other adults, instead hovering around as if waiting for instructions to do something.

Kondie explained, "Polly used ta be a kitchen gin on Big Creek, a cattle station 'bout two hundred miles up north. On that place the blacks lived and ate in their own camp, an' didn't get treated real good. That's why she is a bit jumpy 'bout being here with you."

Both Arthur and his wife nodded their understanding as to why the woman was uncomfortable. They had been around enough to know how the system worked and, while not agreeing with it at times, knew that change would come with time.

The first few weeks in their new town passed quickly for the boys and as veterans of moving and settling into new schools there were few problems that the family had not faced and dealt with in the past.

At most new schools a couple of trips to the area behind the boys' dunny usually established a couple of facts: one was, as individuals the three Tiley boys were more than capable of looking after themselves. The second being that, if necessary, should any situation require it, they became a unit that could deal with most school yard situations.

The school only had forty-four children with fifteen of them coming from two families; the Darcys and the Doolans. These two families were as thick as thieves and if you fell out with just one of them it meant that you had made an enemy of almost half the school.

The headmaster was aware of the situation and kept a close eye on the bigger members of both families to ensure they didn't throw their weight around too much, especially as they were older than others in their class because they had been kept back at some time during their time at school.

This was even worse in the older Tiley's case as Charles had skipped a year and at the age of just eleven was in grade eight. In this school he was in a class with two boys three years his senior.

The school building was low set, which in itself was unusual for Queensland state schools of that era; it had two class rooms, a library and a small office. Both teachers were men which was also not usual. The junior member of staff took grades one to four and the headmaster took five to eight

John was in grade five and had the Darcy twins with him - a year older than him - as well as Shirley Doolan who should have been in grade seven.

The only other kid in his class was the local policeman's daughter Sharon, who, like John, was not local and despite the authority her father held in the town, struggled to be accepted at school.

Girls moving to these small outback towns had a much harder time establishing themselves in the pecking order. They did not have the option of a trip to the back of the toilet block to sort things out as the boys did.

Ceddy, their new-found aboriginal friend, was in grade four and the three brothers had been at the school for almost two weeks before John realised that he never saw him at play times. He literally disappeared. The shy boy would often come over to their place after school but was never around to walk home with them once school was out.

Edward, the youngest of the trio, was in grade one and was therefore in the same half of the school as Ceddy. If it wasn't for him telling them, the older boys would not have known if he was at school or not. This just seemed to be the way it was and the three newcomers were not inclined to rock the boat, especially at this early stage of their settling in.

Even though there was very little or no contact at school, Ceddy soon became a part of the Tiley trio outside school hours, he was the same age as John and soon became his friend; however the bond being established was with the entire family including their parents.

The contrast could not have been more evident, they were all big and blond and he was small, skinny and dark, the Tiley boys' presence could not be missed, while for the better part you never knew Ceddy was around.

One afternoon sitting on the back steps John said, "Come on let's go t' your place t' play for a change."

"I don't have nothin' there, an' you wouldn't like it."

"I reckon I would ya know, I never seen your place but I reckon it would be OK."

Ceddy obviously was not sure but before he had a chance to say no, John was already up and walking in the direction that he had seen Ceddy appear from.

On catching up he said, "I'm an Abo ya know." His blond companion looked him up and down before answering, "Yep, I know. Me Mum told me. Only she used a much longer word, n' said Abo was OK t' say but Boong was not a good word. I don't know why, 'cause its not swearin'."

"I'm a Boong as well as an Abo."

"Does an Abo grow up to be a Boong, like a boy grows up to turn into a man?"

"Naw its just wot white fellas call us."

"I get called Blondie or Snowy by some adults but I don't like it much."

Ceddy looked down at the ground, picked up a stone between his toes and flicked it ahead of them.

"Kondie said you was a real blondie," he said pausing for a moment, "Wot's it mean?"

"It's the colour of me hair, 'n it's like a nick name. But I already got a nick name 'cause me real name is Richard, 'n I think because of an uncle I'm called John, so it's gotta be a nick name don't cha reckon?"

As they neared Ceddy's place he again tried to talk John out of going there, "Er Polly might be cranky if I turn up with you."

"Wot's she gonna be mad about? I won't come in if she goes off, but I reckon if you are me mate we should be able to go to each other's houses."

"Are you an' me mates then?"

"I dunno wot exactly makes a couple of blokes mates, but ya sorta just become mates don't cha reckon?"

"Is that the same if it is a white fella and a black fella, kin they be mates? Kondie bin telling Polly that you gonna git a bunch a trouble fer hanging 'round wid me."

"Me Mum an' Dad don't have no problems, so who 'm I gonna git inta trouble with? Do ya think Polly an' Kondie don't want ya t' be me mate?"

"Nar, they tink yous a good bloke. Ya jest don't know this town."

"Well if ya wanna be me mate, it's a goer, we c'n be mates."

"Us black fellas when we's real mates we are bruthers, do ya wanna be me bruther? Bet cha don't."

John pondered the question for a while then replied "Nah, I got two brothers; ya gotta be born to be a brother, but to be a mate ya gotta be picked an' that makes being a mate special, well t' me anyway."

"I never seen it that way before 'cause we have two sorts of bruthers the blood sort n' the special mate sort." Again John thought carefully about his answer, "All right, " he concluded "I'll be ya brother an' you can be me mate, what d' ya reckon mate?"

Ceddy's face beamed and the ever present grin got even bigger. "Ripper brother, she's a goer, we is bruthers an' mates."

By now they had reached Ceddy's house and without a word about what fallout the visit may or may not create, they marched straight in.

The house was not dissimilar to a lot of camp housing John had lived in and therefore he did not find the sheet iron walls and dirt floor in any way strange, or off putting. The place was a lot cleaner than a lot of camp shacks John had been into, especially in the single men's part of the camp.

Almost as if she was expecting it, Polly was not surprised at their joint arrival; she did however carefully pull the hessian curtain that divided the two room shack.

"G'day, you young fellas. Yous want a cuppa?"

"No thanks Mrs Polly, but kin I have a drink outer ya water bag?"

Polly looked startled at the way John had addressed her but let it ride, then replying, "Yep, use the panikin on the sink; it's clean."

She quietly addressed Ceddy, "You know ya got some jobs to do an' I don't want no aggro 'bout it."

"Arr Aunty me an' John are mates, couldn't I do 'em later 'cause we are going to go to the creek?".

Polly relented and the boys spent the first of many fantastic adventures at Saltwater Creek; one of the tributaries of the Menton River that was within easy walking distance of the town.

Over their brief twelve month friendship this spot on the creek became a special place where they made canoes, fished, crabbed, foolishly swam or just explored. Their future as mates was to be tested in ways that were terribly unfair, but for the better part life was pretty good for two young boys who just revelled in each other's company.

For the entire period of their friendship, John, who thought he was pretty good in the bush, never ceased to be amazed at his friend's scrub know-how. Ceddy taught him how to catch catfish by hand in the mud, what to rub on a wasp sting or the foods you could dig up or pick.

In return the white boy and his family, above all else, taught the black boy to respect himself, his culture and his people. He learnt the importance of going to school and education and just by his association with the family realised that not all white people were the same.

Knowing full well that most of the town's residents had a less than tolerant attitude, Ceddy had steered their friendship out of town to their spot at the creek; for his part the blond member of the duo was blissfully unaware that a certain element in town was not happy with the boys knocking around together and a few had even voiced their displeasure.

Their parents heard the whispers but decided to let the matter lie for the present. However, they knew that sooner or later their sons would become involved one way or another in the racial problems that existed in their new town, but they were also confident that at their level, the boys would be able to deal with the problem.

They were not, however, as confident of their own ability to deal with the problem at an adult level.

So, for the moment things ticked along without any complications, Ceddy at least knew this would last only as long as the boys were away from the town or at the Tileys' house.

John, for his part, was still puzzled by his mate's disappearing act when class came out of school; also, when the bell went to go back into class Ceddy would magically appear again.

One day as soon as class was out for lunch, John grabbed him before he could disappear and insisted that they eat their lunch together and for Ceddy to join the make up game of cricket that was on every day.

The system was that two of the eldest boys picked the sides from anyone that was available and wanted to play at that time. However this day everyone was picked until only Ceddy remained. Ignoring him, the two sides started to walk towards the pitch.

"Hey ya gotta pick Ceddy yet!" said John pointing to his mate.

One of the captains turned to the other and said, "I don't want a Boong on my side, not even sure I want a Boong lover on my side. What d' y' reckon?" he said to the other captain. "Yep, he'll probably spear someone with one of the stumps or use the bat as a nulla nulla," he laughed.

While the three brothers did not fully understand the cruel meaning of what was said, they knew enough, especially in the smart snide way both boys had spoken.

Immediately they drew Ceddy into their formation and as ever Charles took up the verbal challenge, "He goes to this school an' is a pretty good cricketer, better than half the kids here so ya gotta let him play."

The bigger of the two captains stepped forward, "All Boongs should be up at the settlement and not even at this school, so stick that in ya pipe an' smoke it, ya bloody mob of Boong lovers."

Charles tried diplomacy. "Look it's only a game. Seems silly to have a blue over a game don't you think?" John moved next to his brother with Edward a little behind them, yet obviously ready to follow any lead his older siblings gave.

Poor Ceddy was out of his depth, he was like a kangaroo caught in the headlights of a car, not sure what the likely outcome could be and what role he may be expected play.

Above all else he was definitely confused by the stance the brothers had taken on his behalf.

The two groups stared at each other in a Mexican standoff; the Tileys waiting for some sort of response to Charles's question. The others, whose numbers had largely dwindled to the Darcys and Doolans plus a couple of hangers on were just not sure what sort of threat the combination of the three brothers presented, even though the odds were more than three to one in their favour.

Luckily the immediate start of World War Three was averted by the arrival of the Head Master, who had seen the standoff and strode over demanding to know what was going on. The only response he got from both parties was "Nuthin' Sir." Knowing exactly what the problem was, he ordered everyone into class thereby giving things a chance to cool down.

During the course of class that afternoon Charles and the two team captains were taken into his office, here he warned them all, that he "Would not tolerate the sort of behavior he had witnessed in the playground."

Charles tried to explain, "Sir, these kids won't let our mate Ceddy play cricket and we were just stickin' up for him. The lunch time game is for everyone, even the girls can play so I reckon you should tell them Ceddy can too."

The Head Master already knew what the affair was about yet, for some reason, he stopped short of instructing the two senior boys of the school to allow Ceddy to join in the lunch time cricket match.

This lack of leadership was definitely noticed by Charles as later in the day he was to ask the teacher why he had failed to do what the boy knew was the right thing.

To Charles's question the teacher replied, "Look young Tiley, you are new at this school and I didn't do anything because I don't want any trouble." The reply did not in any way satisfy the boy, but he was wise and polite enough not to push the point at that time.

The Head, however, for all his failings, was on the ball enough to keep the brothers in school after three thirty, this naturally would give their adversaries time to get clear of the school hopefully defusing the situation even longer. He also knew that the elusive Ceddy would have enough savvy to be able to avoid any problem that might arise on his way home.

Being kept in for something that was not of his doing seemed unfair to Charles and after a while in detention he decided to ask, "Excuse me Sir, why are we being punished for something that was not our fault and especially as nothing actually happened?"

The Head who was again a little taken aback by the boy's straight forward question, replied, "I felt that both parties were equally to blame for the incident, even though, you are right, nothing did happen and so as to make sure that continued to be the case, I made the decision to keep you lot back for your own good."

The boy persisted, "Sir, we are pretty good at looking after ourselves, but as Ceddy wasn't kept back you should have told Jack and Carl not to touch him." And he added another shot about the cricket, "An' you should have told them to let him play cricket."

He pondered the boy's outburst and, as was his habit, interlocked his fingers into a single fist and thrust it up under his thin pointed chin, forcing his head back and his shoulders up. The brothers waited for what seemed to be an eternity, sure that they or at least Charles was going to cop it, "I would normally punish a kid with four cuts if he spoke to me like that but you have all been kept in for half an hour so that is the end of it." To the boys' amazement he turned and left the room only pausing to add, "You may all go home now."

While it was not unusual for one of the boys, especially John, to be kept in after school, it was most unusual for all three to be disciplined, so when they arrived home their mother knew something was amiss and immediately wanted to know what the problem was. The boys, still a little unsure of the reason for the fracas, told their mother of the entire incident from start to finish.

Knowing her sons' ability to look after themselves her immediate concern was for Ceddy. "Was he kept in as well?" she asked and "Did they know where he was?"

"I saw he just took off as soon as class was out, an' I don't think he was gonna get caught by nobody," said Edward.

Not able to help herself his Mother replied, "Going to get caught by anybody. However, do you think he was upset by what happened?" she continued.

"From what he said as we walked to class I reckon he wasn't scared of the Darcys or the Doolans but more of not being able to be John's mate anymore," said her eldest.

At this point, John spoke for the first time, "Mum, how can these kids talk to Ceddy like they did and not get into strife with their Mum or Dad? That big Doolan kid, Jack, was so angry that he was spitting all over Charles an' me while he was talking, it was like he was crazy, I reckon he should be called Crazy Jack."

"Prejudice is a difficult word to say and even harder to explain especially when it is directed at someone because of their colour, their race or even what church they go to." Wanting to get her explanation over to her sons in a way that wasn't in itself prejudice she bought some time by suggesting a cold Milo drink.

Five minutes later sitting on the back steps savouring their unexpected treat their mother continued, "I guess you are all old enough to know that the way the children behaved at school today was because of what they have heard and seen at home. They have been wrongly told that people like Ceddy, Kondie or Polly aren't as smart, as clean or even as human as white people." Rolling a cigarette their mother frowned in concentration, wanting her words to deliver a message that would be understandable for all three of her sons.

She lit her smoke and sighed in pleasure while exhaling the first lungful, "Being Tileys you all know what an argument is." The three blond heads nodded, knowing full well that both of their parents enjoyed nothing better than a good heated discussion on almost any topic. "Most times when people argue different ideas or feelings are put forward and you think about what was said and agree or not. Even though you may not like what was said you should always listen carefully and try to learn and perhaps take something out of the message being given to you." By this time the cigarette was almost spent, the butt was extinguished on the step and then put into the packet of tobacco, to be later split open and any remaining remnants mixed in with the next cancer stick to be rolled. "The problem," she continued, "is, that a lot of people find it easier just to agree than to question. The parents of some of the kids at school have been told that black people aren't as good as white and instead of asking why. They have just agreed and then sadly passed this rubbish on to their kids."

Not sure she was getting through, Isobel concluded, "Make up your mind on someone because of what you know about them, not because of what you hear or because they may be different to you."

"D' ya reckon it's a bit like the problems we had at the school in Ballon?" asked John.

His mother's mind immediately went back to the difficult time the boys had had at their last school. As parents they had always let the boys sort things out at school for themselves, while interested and involved in the boys learning process, they also accepted that corporal punishment was a part of the normal discipline in schools, but not so long ago their belief in the system had been shaken enough for them to consider an alternative learning establishment, even the local convent school.

At Ballon all of the employees working on the irrigation scheme lived in prefabricated huts down on the bank of the river. There were some twenty of these huts and most of the families had children at the local state school, the men all came from construction backgrounds and, like the Tileys, were used to a transient lifestyle.

To be honest some of these kids were just a bit wild, and some were known to have hydraulic tendencies, that is, they liked to lift things. The locals could accept some indiscretions from their own but from outsiders it was another matter. This, together with normal small town parochial attitudes, meant that any outsiders were viewed as an intrusion that, at best, was to be tolerated. They argued that these intruders interfered with their usual laid back country lifestyle. The fifties was a time of change in Australia, yet change did not come easily to lot of country people.

During the time of this camp, the river kids as they were called, were blamed for anything that was amiss in the town. Yep! If it was stolen, broken or damaged the locals always pointed their fingers in the direction of the river and while the local merchants were more than happy to have the custom of an extra twenty families, their attitude was always one of sufferance. For the better part the river kids kept pretty much to themselves but things became a little more serious when several of the teachers let the town's attitude influence the way they treated any non-local children in class. Caning and lengthy after school detention became an issue that even the parents of the toughest kids could not ignore; this resulted in a group, including Isobel, meeting with the headmaster requesting that something be done.

Nothing came of this delegation except a promise to 'look at things'. From the kids' standpoint *things* probably got worse with the offending teachers now having a personal stake in the vendetta against the children living on the river bank. All concerned had made a point, but that was about it, and with the irrigation contract soon to be completed it seemed a better option to just take their lumps and stay out of trouble as much as possible.

Their time in Ballon was not a happy time for the boys and it was the only time that one of them played the wag. John remembered that day only too well. The day before he wagged it, he had a fight with the headmaster's son and fearing the caning, that sure as hell he was going to get, he and a mate decided to take off for the day and hope that the matter would be forgotten by the time they returned after the weekend.

On that Friday John and his mate, Butch, left for school at the same time as usual but, instead of going on towards the school, they crossed the river, hid their school bags and spent the day swimming, in the nude of course, and exploring the country. When they guessed it was time to head home they went to collect their bags only to realise that they had not made a good enough mental note of where they had hidden them.

At first it was a bit of a game, trying to retrace the foot prints they had made earlier that day. However, it wasn't long before the boys started to become concerned as their ports held not only their school books, both text and work, but their shirts. To arrive home without your port might give some breathing space to search further during the weekend but without a shirt on as well, would certainly take some explaining. As time wore on their search became more and more frantic until, at last, the bags were found.

John arrived home puffed from running and was immediately asked by his mother what he was doing coming home at this hour. It was while trying to explain that he had been kept in again that he looked at the clock on the fridge, aghast he realised that he was home an hour early.

Even though it went against the grain, his parents decided that John's truancy would be dealt with by the school, so on Monday he was taken to class and punished accordingly. The matter was not discussed again other than to ask John what punishment he had received.

On later reflection John often remarked that, "I would like to meet my teacher from that school again to ask him by what right did he think he had to treat the river kids the way he did."

Their time at the camp in Ballon also introduced the boys to the problems associated with domestic violence and when children were at risk Isobel often involved herself in these affrays. From time to time wives and children would take refuge at the Tileys' place while Isobel sorted out the husband. Arthur would use his authority as a foreman but more often than not it was his wife who would stand toe to toe and tell the guy to "Bugger off and come back when you're sober".

Back on the steps of their new home, Isobel looked at the three boys after John had drawn an analogy to Ballon, "Er, yes I suppose it is a bit like that, although in that town, something could have been done but it wasn't. We could have forced a change as the law was on our side. Here, even the law and governments do not feel aboriginals are equal and that is where the real difference lies. Sadly, it will take years and a lot of heartache before the present attitude of igIsobelnce will disappear."

Whether their mother's words were fully understood or not didn't really matter; as with children the world over, they had a happy knack of being able to roll with the punches, making the best of things, and getting on with life.

The next day of school the boys didn't push the idea of Ceddy playing cricket and from his point of view he was content to slip again into the background.

It was a while before the boy again turned up at the Tileys after school and it was on this particular visit that he was introduced to the gloves. He walked into the yard to find Charles and John were sparring under the watchful eye of their mother. While boxing was definitely not a sport that either parent wished the boys to pursue, they did believe that all three should be able to look after themselves. So the boys always had a set of boxing gloves and were encouraged to spar with each other and with any of their friends that wanted to have a go. In fact many school problems had been settled in the Tiley's back yard with Isobel acting as the referee, and these contests did not always include one of her sons and rarely ended with more than bleeding nose and a bruised ego.

"Wotcha letting 'em fight for Missus?" Ceddy asked, a little worried about the proceedings. In his world a fight meant that two or more people were hell bent on hurting each other. Isobel explained, "They are not fighting Ceddy, they are boxing. You see the big gloves they have on their hands?" The boy nodded, "Well the gloves are thick and soft so you can hit each other and it doesn't hurt."

"But missus, if yous in a blue, ya gotta hurt the other bloke cause he sure gonna hurt you if he get a chance. Me cousin-brothers at the settlement tell me don't muck around even if ya hafta use a waddy."

Isobel was interested, "What do you do if someone picks a fight with you at school?"

"I don't like fightin' an' Kondie reckons if I wack a white fella then we could get sent away to a nudder place far away, so at school I just run away."

"Do you have to run away very often?" she asked.

"A while back when I first come to school it use ta be a lot, but none a' them white kids could catch me." He said with a shy laugh. "I'm pretty fast ya know. They reckon I'm a dingo, but I know I'm not. Kondie could fight anybody but he doesn't, he don't run away but just won't fight."

The boy had never engaged in such a lengthy conversation with a white adult before and Isobel was keen to let him keep talking.

"If Kondie said it was alright to learn to box like Charles and John would you like to?"

It was obvious that he was interested but was not sure how to respond. "It looks like fun but would it be alright for a Boong t' do that sorta fightin' with a white fella?"

"Ceddy" Isobel said quite sternly, "Boong is not a nice word for anyone to call you. I know a lot of people do and that Kondie says it, but I would be happy if you did not use it while you are at our place."

She knew immediately that she could have used a different approach to the use of 'Boong' and in an attempt to reassure Ceddy she continued,

"It's not your fault, it's just a bad white fella word used for your people. Now, would you like to try on the boxing gloves?"

By now the boys had finished their bout and Charles offered his gloves to Ceddy. "Go on mate, give John a smack in the ear." He took the gloves and even pulled them on; however no amount of encouragement could entice him to throw a punch in his friend's direction.

Isobel knew that the boy needed to be assured. "Look son," she said, "I will talk to Kondie, but, just to have a try, John will hold out his hands and you try to hit him on the gloves."

The boys danced around with John holding his hands out in front of him and urging Ceddy to hit them, he didn't move them away and very quickly his friend was landing punch after punch into the palms of his gloves.

"Pretty good mate, now I am going to move my hands around a bit an' you see if you can still hit them." Now it became a contest with each trying to score points either by making the other miss or hitting the target. Arthur arrived home during this little contest and was impressed at Ceddy's natural rhythm and hand speed.

He nodded to Isobel and said, "A bit of practice and there won't be too many at school will push him around." His wife explained about the boy's reluctance to actually box to which he said, "I will ask Kondie tomorrow if it is alright if Ceddy can put the gloves on, just with our boys."

These backyard bouts became a regular occurrence and the three boys happily passed on the boxing knowledge their father and mother had given to them. Yes, Isobel was no slouch with the gloves but when the boys boxed with her they could only defend and were not allowed to throw a punch. This soon became Ceddy's favorite game. He would taunt Isobel with a cheeky grin and nimbly sway and move away from any punch that was thrown at him. What he lost in strength he certainly made up for with speed and eyes like an eagle.

These sparring sessions on occasions even attracted a few of the other kids to watch and occasionally some of them would even pull on the gloves. It did not take long for the town to learn of Ceddy's ability with his fists as a result of his sparring with the Tiley boys and sadly this made him more of a target than ever.

Now he was a 'Boong' who could fight but without the guts to have a go. For his part Ceddy was more than happy to avoid any conflict by running rather than fighting.

"I reckon ya could flatten that 'Moonface' Darcy," John said on their way to the creek one afternoon.

"Yep! I reckon I could too," came the reply.

"With a head that big ya couldn't miss."

"I kin do him I know, but then Kondie, Polly n' me 'd get sent to prison for a hundred years."

"Wotcha talking about? I've had plenty a' fights an' didn't go to prison."

"Yeh but you ain't a black fella."

John pondered on this until they reached the creek. "Maybe ya right mate, just knowing in ya self that ya can flatten someone is probably good enough."

At this the subject was dropped, they pulled their canoe from where they had hidden it, climbed in and paddled down the creek and across to the aboriginal settlement on the other side.

The kids here went to the settlement mission school and only came into town on special occasions and when accompanied by someone from the mission. People from the town were not encouraged and rarely visited the settlement; however despite the feeling a lot of the town people had towards those in the settlement, the kids and the adults always treated John as a cousin-brother.

As they walked up the bank from the creek an old bloke with a fish pot said, "You bloody kids better b' watchin' out f' that big bloody croc I seen yesterdee."

"G'day, Mista Jimmy." said John, "Do ya reckon that croc would worry us while we are in our canoe?"

"I don't big note meself Blondie but dis bloke would eat both you kids an' think it was just smoko. Dat ole canoe yous in would be jest like the silver paper on a lollie fir him."

The old man took a half smoked durrie out of his pocket and lit it with a wax head match that he struck on the sole of his boot. "I'm watchin' for the bludger even when I put me pots in. I know he like a bit of black fella but I reckon he love to try some fresh white fella too." He laughed at his own joke as he continued on his way to the river bank.

A few of the settlement boys were playing cricket and yelled for Ceddy

23

and John to join them. No worries about sides here, the newcomers just went to opposite ones. After the game they sat behind one of the humpies in the shade. Having been here a number of times, John knew the boys, and was more than at ease in their company.

"Wot d' you blokes think about this croc that Mista Jimmy seen?" he asked, more than just a little concerned.

One of the boys laughed, "Dat ol' fella been seein' crocs all his life; maybe he's a bit nutty, we seen plenty o' little fellas but not the big one ol' Jimmy sees."

Another of the boys asked John, "Wot you call dat ol' Uncle, mister fer, he blacker dan me?"

"I gotta call all adults mister. It don't matter what colour they are. Mum and Dad say it's because you gotta respect older people."

"We call our older people Uncle; we only call white fellas mister."

The same boy took a couple of cigarettes out of his pocket. "You want a durrie mate?" he asked John.

Now, both John's parents smoked and like most boys he had pinched one and had a drag. He didn't particularly care for the experience, he also knew that Ceddy occasionally nicked one of Kondie's so he replied, "Me a' Ceddy 'll share one."

The boy broke all the cigarettes in half and handed them out asking who had a match. Ceddy did and soon all four were sucking on their half durries and if their smoking was observed by any of the adults certainly no body took any notice which was a new experience for John.

Now, while the boys showed a certain amount of bravado with regard to whether or not there was a large croc lurking nearby, when the time came to head for home they quietly decided to walk their canoe about half a mile down the inlet. Here the water was only about seventy five yards wide and the theory was that they would be across before the croc had a chance to react.

"D'ya reckon we'll be right mate?" John asked nervously.

"I'm a Boong but I don't know nothing about crocs."

"You called yourself a Boong again." Ceddy was reminded, "But 'cause we gotta get back, if you're game then we'll give it a go."

The boys climbed into their corrugated iron craft and, with great trepidation, set out for the opposite bank. Their usual practice was to rest several times and bail out their not-so-watertight vessel. However, as every shadow, ripple or unidentified object turned into a man-eating monster, the thought of being stationary never crossed their minds. They reached the opposite bank with an inch of free board to spare and probably in some kind of world record time. Ceddy tapped his mate on the shoulder and, with a grin, said "You might be a white fella but you paddle like a scared black fella."

"Well, you were gettin' whiter an' whiter ya know."

Laughing, the boys pulled the canoe up the bank. "I reckon no water come in 'cause we was goin' too fast".

Over the time of their friendship John and Ceddy spent many afternoons in the bush together and while all the Tileys felt they were pretty good bushmen, John soon realised that when survival was a necessity and not just something you played at, it was very different game.

CHAPTER TWO

CONSEQUENCES

**"In Nature there are neither rewards nor
punishment – only consequences."
RoEdward Green Ingersoll 1833-1899**

The next few months were pretty quiet with the Tileys enjoying their
new school, but the situation with Ceddy was never far from the surface.
The boys were smart enough to know they couldn't change things, so for
the time being they were more than happy to let sleeping dogs lie.

Quite a few of the kids at school accepted John's friendship with
Ceddy and while they did not make any issues about it, they certainly
made it clear there would be no crossing of the line to stand up against
the influence of the Darcy and Doolan children, and this was accepted by
the brothers without any bad feelings.

It was during this uneasy truce that John ran into the family's first real problem. There was a game of marbles going on at the back of the school yard when Ceddy raced up to tell him that Barry Doolan was picking on Edward.

Now, Barry was a grade ahead of John and while not a big kid, he should not have been fighting Edward. While the fight, if you call it that, had not progressed past a bit of pushing and shoving, the thought that a boy older then himself was picking on Edward made John do his block and he reacted in a normal, protective, older brother way.

As soon as young Doolan realised that John was on his way from the back of the school yard he decided that the headmaster's office was the safest place for him at that particular moment. He had barely made it to this relative safety when he was collared by his pursuer. Initially shocked by the intrusion, the headmaster leapt up and pulled the boys apart.

"What the hell do you think you are doing?" he shouted.

John pulled up with a start, suddenly realizing where he was. He let go of Barry and, stammering replied,

"S-s-sorry s-s-Sir it was just, er I was just er ... sorry Sir."

"What have you got to say for yourself, you damn ruffian?"

"Well, Sir, he was fighting with my brother an' he's a lot bigger an' older an' I'll get him 'cause that's what big brothers do."

At this the cane was produced and, using it like a military swagger stick the head circled the two boys.

"Respect!" he spat at John. "That's what you lack Tiley. You think you can do whatever you like, but you are going to learn that that is not the case."

"I am sorry I run into your office, Sir, but what he did was wrong an' he should be in trouble 'cause Edward's only a little kid."

The cane left a vivid red welt across John's bare leg, "Don't you dare talk to me like that boy, I will decide what is right and what is wrong." With that the cane left another welt a little lower than the first, John rubbed the spot only to be rewarded with a crack across the knuckles.

"Stand up straight," he was ordered.

Barry Doolan had remained silent through the encounter between John and the Head but now it was his turn. "What have you got to say for yourself Doolan?"

"Well, Sir, his brother swore at my little sister an' I just gave him a little push t' tell him not to swear in front of girls."

John interjected, "That's bull Doolan, Edward doesn't even swear at all."

"Until you are asked to speak you will keep your mouth shut."

"But, Sir, you..."

"I said keep it shut Tiley," snarled the Head emphasising the point with another swish of the cane. "Carry on Doolan."

"Well, Sir, I seen John comin' an' I know he can fight Sir, so I run up here so he couldn't get me Sir."

"I can understand that, boy; you go and ring the bell for class." Smirking at John, Barry left the room but with John's words following him.

"I'll get ya Doolan," a comment that brought another swish of the cane and another grunt of pain.

"Now Tiley, what have you got to say, and I warn you boy, be careful."

"I told you Sir, he was picking on Edward. I'm sorry I run into your room, Sir, but I will get him, 'cause wot he said is a lie."

"What you will get is six of the best in front of the class." To indicate that he wanted the boy to move to the class room John was given a swipe across the seat of his pants with the cane. Now, as luck, either good or bad depending on who you were, would have it, as a child John suffered quite badly from boils and at this particular time had a rather nasty one on his upper thigh that was hidden by his shorts. As he followed the Head into the class room he could feel the blood running down his leg, whether through pigheadedness or an attempt at martyrdom he didn't say a word about the injury. The Head addressed the class.

"Tiley has ideas that he is running the school, however as I am a fair man his punishment will be reduced if we all receive an apology from him for his bad behavior." At this he nodded at John, "Well what have you got to say for yourself?"

"As I said before, I apologise to you, Sir, but I will not say sorry to Doolan an' he better watch himself this arvo after school." came the reply. This was not the answer expected and the Head's reaction was swift and for John painful. The cane fell three times with exact precision on each hand with the class wincing with each stroke. "Now go to my office and reconsider your answer."

All eyes followed John's painful exit from the room with one child exclaiming loudly, "Oh yuck! Look at the blood runnin' down his leg."

John continued to the office but was only there a minute or so before the Head came in, "What happened to your leg?" he demanded.

"You bust me boil Sir."

"Rubbish boy you must have banged it on the desk or door."

"No Sir. It bust when you gave me that last whack with the cane when we were in your office."

The teacher was clearly worried about the boil but refused to accept responsibility and continued to push for the result he wanted in regards to the clash in his office.

"I am still waiting for an apology then we can sort out your boil problem."

"I apologise to you Sir but I will get him this arvo," was what he got again.

"You are a glutton for punishment boy, hands out," and the cane fell again this time only twice on each hand.

John was determined not to show how much he was hurting and struggled to stop the tears from running down his cheeks, "Sir, can I check my boil?" the boy asked pulling up leg of his shorts, revealing a mess of blood and puss seeping from under the dressing his mother had put on before school.

"Why did your mother let you come to school with a boil like that?"

"It wasn't bust before, but now it is. I gotta bathe it with hot water to get the heads out or it will be a real problem, an' someone has t' give it a squeeze. My Mum can do it but she went with Dad t'day."

The Head was in a quandary; on one hand he was concerned about any repercussion regarding the actual bursting of the boil but he was also genuinely concerned for the boy's health and then there was the original problem of the fracas in his office.

"Look," he said, "If I get the first aid box do you think you could clean up your leg? You can, er, do it in the office here and I'll get Charles to give you a hand."

Both the boys were accustomed to dealing with boils and while it looked a mess it only took Charles a few minutes to clean it up.

"You want me to give it a squeeze, mate?" he asked, "I reckon she'll pop a beauty."

John raised his eyebrows and looked at his brother. "An' it'll hurt like a cow, I know how you squeeze."

"What sort of baby are you; my giving it a bit of a squeeze'll be better than Mum sticking a hot bottle on it."

John considered his brother's offer, "OK, give 'er a go, but if I say stop you stop."

Once he started and despite his brother's moans of pain, he kept pressure on the boil until he was sure all the heads were out.

He cleaned it up with antiseptic, then, as he had seen his mother do on many occasions, he made a wick out of bandage material. This he pushed it into the hole the boil core had left in his brother's leg. The wick would keep the wound open and let the boil drain completely. "There she is, mate, as good as Mum could have done."

The boys had not seen the Head standing at the door watching the procedure, and Charles continued "What's gonna happen about you goin' t' job Doolan in here?" Unaware they were being overheard John answered, "I dunno, I said I was sorry t' Mr. Brolin but I think he wants me to say I won't give Doolan a hidin' after school."

"Well, why don't cha just let it go, an' maybe he will just accept you saying sorry to him."

"Naw, that way Doolan gets off picking on someone half his size, but if he's got the guts we can put the gloves on at home. Maybe ol' Brolin will think that's OK."

At this point the Head made his presence known, "I do not think that will be OK, young Tiley." he announced "I just want you to forget about any kind of pay back that you feel you owe Barry Doolan. The quicker you understand and accept that, the quicker this matter will be over."

Charles quickly looked at his brother and from the set of his jaw feared the response the Head was going to get.

"If Doolan gets the cuts for picking on Edward then I'll call it square, Sir."

The Head spluttered, "I am not here to bargain with you boy, stay in my office while you reconsider, especially as the boil you were dying from seems to have magically cured itself." Nodding that Charles was to accompany him, the Head left the room. During the remainder of the afternoon he made regular visits to the office, but, despite his sore hands and bleeding boil John was adamant that one way or the other Barry Doolan should be punished for what he had done.

After school he kept John standing in the corner of his office until his day's paperwork was done and he himself wanted to go home.

"Tiley," he said, "I give you this warning. If I hear of any problems that can be vaguely related to this issue between you and Doolan, there will be hell to pay I can promise. Now get your gear and take off."

John didn't wait to be told twice and was home within ten minutes where his mother was waiting his arrival. "How is your boil?" she asked first up.

"A bit sore, but Charles got most of the gunk out an' I reckon she'll be jake now."

"You better give me a look anyway," and in saying this indicated that John should pull up the leg of his shorts. She lifted the dressing that Charles had applied and grunted her approval of the job he had done. "Very good, a bit bruised from the cane but no real damage done. Now, I want you to tell me what happened at school today."

John knew that he would not be able to dodge his Mother's questions and he related in detail exactly what had happened.

When he was finished she asked, "What are you going to do now?"

Without hesitation John replied, "I told Mr. Brolin I was sorry that I come into his room, but I also said I would get Doolan for picking on Edward an' I reckon I will."

Isobel pondered on his reply before saying "You think very carefully about what you do and what the consequences of your actions might be."

"Yep, I know Brolin will give it to me, but I don't reckon the rest of the Doolan mob will do anything, though if they want to, I'll just have to look out." His mother felt for her son, and certainly did not want him to feel there was any shame in just letting the matter rest. "It may be better if you just let things cool down for a while and sort things out with the Doolans later on."

"I dunno, he's a dingo that Doolan an' he picks on a lot of kids smaller then he is. Old Boiling knows but won't do a thing."

"What if Dad or I have a yarn to Mr. Boiling, do you think that would be enough?"

John scratched his blond head drawing circles in the dust with his big toe. "I'll give it a bit of a go."

"Good for you, and tomorrow Dad or I will talk to Mr. Brolin."

While he was pleased that he wasn't in trouble for what had happened at school, he was still not happy and needed some time to think things out. "Kin I go to the creek for a while?" he asked, knowing that the creek was usually out of bounds on a school day.

To his surprise Isobel answered "Be home before your father and don't get that boil dirty or wet." Then she walked into the house.

John contemplated calling on Ceddy but then decided to spend the last shilling of his pocket money on lollies before going to his mate's place.

The local store sold everything from hardware to clothes to groceries and of course lollies. There was a café in the main street but John preferred the store. The owner, Mr. Daws, was one of his favourite locals and the store was full of wonderful things, so much so that with his eyes closed the boy could almost tell where he was by the delicious smells given off by the different goods for sale.

"Well, what can I do for you, young Tiley?" he was asked.

"I would like six pence worth of raspberries please Mr. Daws." John said, having revised his budget on his way to the store. As the shopkeeper busied himself counting out the little red sweets he asked, "How's school going?" Not sure if Mr. Daws was aware of the day's events John replied "Pretty good, but we get lots of home work."

"Aw! So Brolin's a bit of a slave driver, eh?"

His reply was interrupted by the arrival of Barry and younger brother Chris Doolan. John took his change, "Thanks Mr. Daws." he said, muttering to Barry as he passed, "I'll be waiting outside for ya."

To John's surprise Barry said to the shop keeper, "He's gonna bash me up Mr. Daws."

However, the little shopkeeper had watched the Doolan family bully the town for years and was not about to intercede on Barry's behalf, "You're big enough and ugly enough to look after yourself, Barry." he said, making a joke of the lad's request for help. John waited quite some time for the brothers to appear from the store. "Hey Doolan!" he called, "You are a big man picking on the smaller kids. Well, I'm smaller and younger then you so come on you gutless wonder."

"I'm not gonna fight you, Collie Flower, cause you've learnt boxing an' that means it's not fair."

"Wot did you call me?" said John advancing to an arm's length from the two other boys. Barry knew full well that he had made a mistake by using a nick name that he knew John disliked. "If ya punch me I'll tell Mr. Brolin t'morra" he said, shrinking away from John.

"I reckon ya gonna tell him anyway so I might as well job ya: that way at least I'll be gettin the cane for doin' something." At that he gave the bigger Doolan a shove, and in trying to evade what he presumed was coming next he collided with his brother who had also decided it was time to take evasive action. Both finished up in an untidy heap on the ground but largely unhurt. As John dragged Barry to his feet by his shirt front, buttons came off and the material ripped. "You've ripped me shirt!" he said, tears starting to run down his cheeks. John looked down at the damaged attire and knew that he was going to be in trouble and, immediately deciding not to make the matter any worse, he released Barry.

"You're not worth the sweat Doolan, but you just remember, touch my brother again an' I'll knock your block off, you big cry baby." With one last shove of contempt John walked away down the path between the store and the house next door. As he passed the back door of the shop, it opened and Mr. Daws appeared with a large brown bottle in his hand. "John!" he called, "I got this soft drink with the label gone. I think its Cherry Cheer but without knowing exactly what it is I can't sell it. You can have it if you want."

"Gee that's bonza Mr. Daws. I can clean up the rubbish out here in the back for it."

"That's fair enough I reckon; just put it all in that big box and head off when you are finished. See you lad."

John finished the work fairly quickly and decided to go to Ceddy's place and share the spoils with him. As he walked along, he casually checked the bottle to see if it was his favourite Cherry Cheer. The colour was right and then he noticed that it was clear that the label had been recently pulled off. He was wondering why the shop keeper would do that when he reached the gate of his mate's place. Dulcie was sitting on the verandah smoking a cigarette. "G'day Missus Polly. Is Ceddy around?"

"G'day Blondie", she replied, "Nah, he's gorn off in the truck with Kondie."

"Thanks Missus, I reckon I better be gettin' home."

"Good o' Blondie. I'll be seein' ya."

The walk home gave John time to think about the trouble he was going to be in the next day at school. To give himself just a little more time he sat under a tree and, using the bottle opener on his pocket knife, he opened his soft drink. It was no longer cold and because it had been shaken, the contents sprayed everywhere as the cap came off. In an attempt to reduce his losses John quickly shoved the bottle in his mouth. This resulted in John ingesting Cherry Cheer at a greater rate than even his system would allow. It came out around the lip of the bottle as well as his nose. He coughed and spluttered until he finally had things under control. He then took a long drink from the bottle, slapped the cap back on, then popped a couple of raspberry lollies into his mouth, "Well I better go in and tell Mum" he said to no one in particular.

Isobel and Arthur were both in the kitchen when John came in. "Mr. Daws gave me a bottle of Cherry Cheer for clearing up his yard." he told them immediately in case they were wondering where he got the drink from. "I'll put the rest in the 'fridge 'cause I didn't drink much so everyone can have some". By their faces and the lack of conversation, John knew that something was going on. Arthur was the first to speak "Your mother thought you said that you were going to let this thing with Barry Doolan drop."

"I was gonna."

"Going to, not gonna" corrected his mother.

"Well, I was going to let him off, but when he came into Mr. Daws I just sorta carried on from when we were in Brolin's office. I didn't bash him ya know: I gave him a push n' him and Chris bumped heads. His shirt got ripped an' he started cryin' so I just went."

"We have already heard from Mrs Doolan about the shirt, and according to her you head butted Barry".

"That's a lie ... err! What's a head butt?"

"We are not too worried about what went on at the store and we understand your standing up for Edward, but you have to understand that the action you took today will cause you some grief."

"I know ol' Brolin will give me heaps t'morra but I reckon that's OK, an' I'm not worried about the Doolan kids, but their mum's a real dragon".

Here Isobel spoke, "I told Mrs. Doolan about Barry fighting with Edward and I will fix up his shirt: not that I have to, but I will. No, what you have to deal with yourself is the head master, he is your problem, on your own."

Once John knew that he wasn't going to be punished by his parents his reply was an easy one to make. "I can take what ol' Brolin gives me an' I know now the Doolans will back off a bit, so it might be worthwhile."

Secretly Isobel and Arthur were quite proud of the stand John had taken on his brother's behalf and understood how much strength their three boys drew from each other.

The next day started badly for John at assembly. After the anthem was sung the Head addressed the kids, "Will John Tiley come to the verandah," were his first words for the day. The short walk and three steps up seemed like a mile to the ten year old, reaching the teachers he stuttered "Y-y-yes Sir".

"Boy! You knew that if there was any follow on from yesterday's trouble you would be in strife. Is that correct?"

John realised that here in front of the entire school was neither the time nor place to put his side of the story. His experience also told him that by simply accepting his punishment was making a statement to the school, that the Tileys stand up for each other no matter what the consequences.

Nodding his agreement with what the Head said, he stood to attention awaiting his fate. Mr. Brolin first went into the schoolroom, reappearing almost immediately with his cane. "Hand out boy. You know the drill."

John turned his back to the assembly and extended his right hand in front of him, however the teacher was not having that. "You will face the school when taking your punishment." He said, "This way everyone can see that disobeying my orders to is a painful course to follow."

Even though he was quite young and generally very well behaved, John had been given the cane many times. He knew how to hold his hand in a way that the cane would slide off and to move his arm down a little on impact to cushion the blow just a bit. Most teachers were aware of these maneuvers and adjusted the offending hand accordingly. To John's surprise this did not happen and, while the punishment looked bad, the middle Tiley was in no doubt that he had been let off lightly.

Later he told Charles, "I reckon Broling backed off a bit when he gave me the cuts. He didn't straighten me hand or even push me arm down an' the last two were pretty soft." To which his brother replied, "He was probably still feeling a bit bad about whacking you on the boil yesterday." John went over the day's events, "The Doolan kids were pretty quiet today. I dunno 'bout that mob, maybe they are just going to let things settle down, but I wouldn't trust any of them, so we all better watch out." Charles nodded in agreement and the two of them set off for cricket practice, where all animosity between the group was forgotten in their quest to be the best team at the inter town sports in a few weeks. The two older Tiley's were in the team with Charles a very good fast bowler and John the wicket keeper, probably because he was the only one with enough nerve to keep when his brother was bowling.

The weeks up to the interschool sports passed without any trouble and the influence the three had on the overall success during that long weekend certainly improved their standing at the school and the community in general. The only blot on that period was Ceddy's refusal to try out for any of the sports, even though the Tileys and the boy himself, both knew that no one in his age group could run or jump like he could.

Both John and Charles on a number of occasions had asked their friend to participate in the try-outs, only to be told, "I don't wanna be the only black fella there. At school it's OK, I know the rules, but with a bunch of other kids I'd be too scared." By now the boys had a pretty good understanding of the town's prejudice towards Ceddy. What they couldn't fully go along with was the way that Ceddy accepted this attitude as if it was normal. Because of their short association with the boy they would never understand that his young life had already conditioned their mate not to buck the system or present himself as a target, this way he was a lot less likely to get hit.

With the interschool athletic and cricket out of the way the boys turned their attention to the school swimming carnival. Their father had been a champion swimmer as a child, with some saying he could have been another Andrew 'Boy Charlton' had he been able to apply himself.

Because he had not been given the chance to continue with his swimming after primary school Arthur was keen for the boys to excel at his chosen sport; an action that was later to build a barrier between him and John that took years to dismantle.

From their hours spent at the river or creek John knew that Ceddy should definitely be in the swimming carnival, however as with the athletics he was having trouble convincing him to join in.

"Aw come on mate." he insisted "At least just come down to training and you will see that it's OK."

Even though he had lived in town since he started school, Ceddy had never been to the town pool and despite John's assurances he was dubious. "I dunno. I heard one of the settlement kids went there once an' he got a kick in the backside."

"Me mum will be there so I don't reckon anybody is gonna give you a kick anywhere." He was definitely curious about the pool so, against his better judgment said, "Tomorra I'll come wid ya: just t' give it a go."

"Beauty! It'll be bonza you'll see."

The next afternoon, true to his word, Ceddy appeared as the boys got ready to go to swimming training. "Wot do I wear to the swimmin' pool, Missus?" he asked Isobel. She had anticipated this, should Ceddy decide to join them. "Here is an old pair of togs that John has grown out of. You can have them."

"Togs? Wot are togs Missus?"

"It's just another name for pants that are specially for wearing swimming," she replied.

"I think it'll feel funny wearing clothes when you're swimmin'. I never done that before."

Isobel wondered if Ceddy's lack of knowledge concerning white men's swimming etiquette was the reason he was still uncomfortable about coming with them to the pool. Sadly, for all concerned, within half an hour she was to discover first hand just why indigenous children were never seen at the pool.

The boys arrived at the pool ready to go straight in, which they did. Ceddy hung back and came in with Isobel, who, this particular afternoon was taking the squad as Arthur was out of town. Some of the children were yet to arrive so she instructed the group "We will start the day on the kick boards and those of you who do not have one can practice your kicking by just hanging on to the edge of the pool." Then turning to Ceddy she said "Come on, get in and grab John's board. All you do is hang on to it and kick up and down the pool with the other kids." He did as he was asked, but was clearly apprehensive about entering the water. Once in, he soon got the hang of using the kick board and joined in the fun.

The session had been underway for only a short while when a car pulled up with the two Snider children both of whom came to training only occasionally. The driver of the car was their father and the Chairman of the Council that employed Arthur. The boy and girl, like most, had come dressed in their togs and with a wave to those already there jumped straight in. Their father took some mail from the dash of his car, quickly scanned the envelopes for importance before returning them to the dash and he then followed his children into the pool enclosure.

Dressed in smart shorts and long white socks, almost the standard dress for white collar workers of that era, he walked with the manner of someone accustomed to others stepping aside to let him pass. The man himself was in his early thirties, short, thickset and balding, with piercing blue eyes that scanned the pool as if checking that those there were worthy of his children's presence. At first glance nothing seemed amiss. It was only when his eyes grew accustomed to the glistening bodies did Ceddy's presence register with him. "What is that bloody Boong doing in the pool?" he screamed. "George, Gloria get out of the water immediately and don't go near that bloody Boong."

The children pulled themselves from the pool and stood on the edge with their hands clutched in front of them waiting for further instructions from their father, who now turned to Isobel. "How dare you bring that black bastard to a pool where ordinary people swim. You buddy up to the Boongs if you want, but you have no right to put other children at risk from disease and other things." Isobel's face should have told the man to shut up but, like the fool he was, he poked his finger at her saying, "My Council has a law that forbids blacks from using facilities like the pool and that law is there because they don't understand about hygiene like we do". At this point Isobel took hold of the jabbing finger, "Take your finger out of my face or I will break if off. As for you quoting Council law at me, I am sure you and your racist Council may have a law forbidding people from the settlement from using the town pool." Having backed off to a safe distance the Chairman interjected, "So you knew it was illegal yet you still dared to bring that dirty bugger here." Isobel bristled. "That boy is as clean or cleaner than your children, plus he has probably never in his life been subjected to the type of rubbish and filth that has come from your mouth today. Also, for your information Mister Snider, Ceddy is not under the Aboriginal Act so even you and your red neck mates can't stop him from using the pool."

Having gathered their things and left by the other gate the two children were standing by the car when their father made his passing shot, "Your old man had better watch his P's and Q's. One mistake and his feet won't touch the ground". Isobel knew full well the meaning in his words but still said, "What a grubby little creep you really are and don't ask your children what they thought of your display today as they may shock you with the truth."

Even though the incident had upset her Isobel completed the training secession, sadly, without Ceddy. The boy was naturally disturbed and as soon as the verbal exchange started had gone behind the change rooms, climbed the back fence and cleared out. Before the remaining children left Isobel spoke briefly to them, "I am sorry about what happened today and if any of your parents would like to talk to me about it please tell them to drop by the house."

On the way home John asked, "Can I go to Ceddy's place for a while just t' make sure he's jake?" His mother nodded her agreement but as usual added something, "Make sure you are home before your father and your homework gets done."

His mate was sitting on the front steps carving a piece of wood when John arrived. He looked up and smiled as his friend approached, "Gees mate I thought your old lady was gonna smack Snider, she done her block good an' proper I reckon."

"Yeah she got a bit agro alright, she said t' say sorry to ya for what happened."

"She don't have t' be sorry, she's a ripper your mum. It don't bother me that people don't like Boongs an' shout bad things. Kondie, he reckons that the problem belongs ta them white fellas not me, so I just run away an' laugh to meself."

On his way home John pondered on Ceddy's attitude and decided that at times he could take a leaf out of his friend's book. When he brought up the subject at dinner that night it was obvious that more than one family member felt it would be a good idea if they used a little more tact at times.

The pool incident passed with very little being said by either side and the boys were surprised by the lack of attention it drew at school. Perhaps if the truth be known the shire Chairman was even lower than the Tileys on the town's social and popularity ladder.

The school swimming carnival went ahead without Ceddy and Isobel's help. The boys did swim, however, and won every event they entered. There was certainly no argument as to which side of the family their aquatic talents came from. Born in England, Arthur was brought to the wilds of North Queensland in nineteen twenty one. Here the family initially settled at Mission Beach and Arthur, together with his sister Joy, took to the water like ducks. When he was sent off to boarding school it was thought that 'the little pommy kid' would be another Andrew 'Boy' Charlton, who was Australia's swimming champion of that era. Sadly, his father's ill-health and the start of the depression years, forced the young Tiley out of school to work with his father who, at that time, was doing survey work for the Main Roads Department.

Arthur never commented on what could have been, but made it clear that should any of his children wish to become swimmers they would receive his full support.

Other than swimming for his regiment, Arthur never swam competitively again after leaving school but it was to play a big part in his life a good few years later. The man was competitive in most things, not overly so, but he did enjoy a good argument. Politics and religion were his favourite subjects and he was even known to invite door-knocking Jehovah's Witness couples inside. It's said that these poor people often left the house totally confused and even questioning their faith. He was in fact a very Christian man but with only one problem, he didn't believe in God. He felt that churches had taken what was a perfectly good set of moral values and used them to set up their own power base.

There were a number of clergy that he included in the family's circle of friends ranging from Catholic priests to a rabbi and he didn't miss out his friend Shorty who was 'a goat rider', the name given to members of the Masonic Lodge. Despite his, and, for that matter, Isobel's attitude towards religion the boys were encouraged to go to Sunday school and to make up their own minds about God and the church.

This attitude of giving their sons the right to ask questions was very evident in the current difficulties regarding their friendship with Ceddy. Both parents were determined that their own feelings would have as little influence as possible on any relationship the boys had formed or would form in the future.

The family lived comfortably and within their means, but to put a little more into the family coffers Arthur occasionally did a bit of surveying work on the weekends. Most times when sport allowed, he took John with him to work as his chainman. His job was to carry and place the staff so his father could take ground level measurements that would enable water to flow from a bore along a drain in order to water stock. This was an extremely inefficient way of delivering water, however the supply seemed endless so nobody worried about what was happening to the artesian basin miles below the earth's surface.

It was on one of these weekend work trips that John learned a lesson in honesty that was to stay with him for life.

The little Austin bumped across the paddock towards an old drilling rig which was sinking a new artesian water bore. As they pulled up the man operating the unit waved to Arthur and signaled to them to join him for a cuppa.

"G'day Arthur how's it goin' mate? Just made a billy of tea."

"Love one George," came the reply. "How close are you to reaching water?"

As Arthur poured jet black tea from a billy can that was standing in the coals at the edge of the fire, George told him, "Woulda been casing her by now but had two broken cables; second one flipped and me offsider lost the top off his thumb. Not only did I have to splice two cables but I had to take me bloody mate into town. Then the flying quack took him to Townsville."

"What about old Missus Blake? She been going crook about the hold up?" Arthur asked.

"Yeh, she's been havin' a whinge, but that is just the way she is. I've done a lot of work for her over the years and she hasn't changed a bit. Even before old Max got hisself smashed up by that black stallion she was the boss."

The driller pushed his battered hat back on his balding head and lit himself a cigarette. This action drew John's attention to the battered hands lighting the match. The fingers were bent and gnarled with at least two of them missing to the first knuckle. These hands told of a life of extreme physical labour in one of the most demanding and dangerous jobs in the outback. When he stood up his back never straightened and by his walk one leg appeared to be a little shorter than the other.

As the two men stood there smoking and chewing the fat their attention was drawn to another vehicle approaching the rig site. "Bloody hell." said the old timer. "Speak of the devil an' sure as shootin' she'll turn up." A large black car stopped in a cloud of dust with the driver alighting immediately the dust had cleared.

An elderly woman, wearing jeans, checked flannel shirt, elastic sided riding boots and a hat that had certainly seen better days, strode straight up to the two men.

"Mornin' George. G'day Arthur. Thought I heard a strange vehicle a while back."

Arthur extended his hand 'Morning Missus Blake. Yeah we only got here a while back". She accepted the offered hand and told him sternly, "The boy can call me Missus but to you I am Gloria."

"No worries, Gloria, this is my son John. Son, this is Missus Blake."

"Pleased t' meet. Missus Blake" said John shaking hands with the sheep cocky surprised at the strength in her grip. To his embarrassment she said to his father, "Good looking kid, Arthur. I'll bet the sheilas all love that blond hair." John looked pleadingly at his father as if requesting him to end this particular conversation. Arthur recognised his son's predicament and answered, "At the moment he is more interested in football and cricket than girls."

"Give him a couple of years and that will change." Then changing the subject, "Damn I forgot to bring the survey pegs up with me. Maybe I was concerned about putting them in this useless bloody car we bought."

"Not to worry, take my car. John can go with you. He can do all the lifting and carrying."

In the car and bumping along the track back to the homestead, John was asked "So what grade are you in Blondie?"

Normally John did not like to be called Blondie but the way the woman spoke it seemed very natural, not annoying him as usual. He replied, "Grade five."

Even though diplomacy was not her high suit she was curious enough to inquire "Big bloke for grade five aren't ya?"

John knew she was suggesting that maybe he had been keep kept back and he was keen to set the record straight. Like it or not there was a stigma attached to children who could not keep up in school.

"Everyone says all us Tiley's are big for our age. I'm only ten but me brother Charles is twelve an' he's in grade eight."

The station owner knew that John's answer had been carefully worded so as not to be cheeky but to let her know that he was not behind at school and in fact his older brother was ahead of where he should have been. Smiling to herself she continued the conversation, "Are you going to be a surveyor like your old man?"

John considered his answer. "Naw, I don't think so. I like to pull things to bits but I'm not much good at putting 'em back together. So I reckon if I become a mechanic, then I'll learn properly how to put things back together as well."

"Good idea boy, the country will always be looking for mechanics so you'll never be short of a quid that's for sure."

At this point the conversation took a turn that John did not expect, "I hear you and old Kondie's grandson are good mates. You must get a bit of stick at school for that."

"Yeh, that's Ceddy. He's me mate. He's black ya know, an' a lot of people in town don't like black people. Not because they don't like 'em. It's just because they are a different colour."

"What does your old man think of you being friends with, er what's his name?"

"His name is Ceddy. My Mum an' Dad don't care if someone is black. They reckon ya can knock around with anyone who is a good bloke."

"Good on your Mum and Dad. I wish there were a few more like that in town." She slowed the car while some sheep cleared the road. "If God made any animal more stupid then sheep I am yet to see them." She paused before continuing, "I went to school with Kondie you know, right here on the station."

John was surprised at this revelation and asked, "How did ya have enough kids out here for a school?"

"Well back when I was a kid there were four families working on this station. I have three brothers and two sisters and there were usually seven or eight kids from the other families. With that many Dad hired a teacher and built a small class room and accommodation for the teacher behind the big house. We did all our primary schooling in that school. We also had a camp of blacks and my father always encouraged any of the kids from there to come up and join us."

"So Kondie came over from the camp did he".

"No, he came from somewhere up the river. He had gone to a mission school but when it closed he came down to ours."

"So did his Mum an' Dad work here when he went to the school?"

The car stopped at the gate for the house paddock. John was out in a shot and swung it open. "Leave it open until we go back to the rig." he was told.

Getting back into the car John was keen to hear more about Kondie, "So did you know Kondie's Mum and Dad?"

"You know John I never thought about his parents. They may have been in the camp but they didn't work here. For more than two years that boy never missed a day at school."

"Wow! He must have had a pretty strict teacher?"

She smiled at John's reply. "Actually his teacher was my Aunt Carol and she was a very easy going person. You don't understand, Kondie didn't have to go to school, he wanted to. In the two years he was here he did four years work and completed grade eight. My Aunt Carol reckoned it was because she was a brilliant teacher but the truth is that Kondie had a great thirst for knowledge."

"You know my Dad reckons he's a gentle giant and a pretty smart bloke who doesn't want people to know that he is. That's funny don't ya reckon?"

"Well, I think your father is right but, while it may seem strange that Kondie wants to hide that he is smart, I can understand why he does."

By this time they had reached the station house and John was out immediately to start loading up the marker pegs. "You stack them in son." he was told, "And I will make a thermos of tea to take back with us."

"This is a bloody great little car your old man's got young fella." John was informed as he climbed back in after shutting the house paddock gate on their return journey.

A little surprised by the statement, but with more than a little pride he answered. This car has got as much power as forty big horses. It can carry Mum and Dad, us three kids and a lot of gear. She's good in mud 'cause she's light an' powerful, but the electric spark thing doesn't work if you go through a lot of water."

The woman laughed. "A car salesman who tells the truth, now that's a switch. Can you drive this car".

"Yep, I can drive Dad's ute too, but this car is much easier."

"Did you see the car I drove up in?"

"Did I ever? She's a beauty. This car is an Austin too you know, but it must be the baby sister of the one you drive. I saw it is called a Princess an' I bet it cost a few quid."

"My husband bought it and you are right it did cost a few quid, but it isn't a very practical car to have on a station, better something like this little beauty."

The rest of the day John was busy putting in pegs and holding the staff for his father to take readings. By sundown they had laid out the path the bore drain would take for about the first two miles and, as gravity was the water's only means of movement, the accuracy of the survey was very important.

As the Tileys packed away their equipment Missus Blake and her husband Max arrived in the Austin Princess. She got out and asked, "How did it go Arthur?"

"Pretty good I think. I have managed to get the line quite close to that clump of trees you pointed out this morning."

"That's ideal as we want to put a couple of troughs near those trees later. Oh, Arthur come and meet my husband, Max. Excuse him not coming over but he doesn't get around so well since his accident a while back." Arthur walked over to their car where Max Blake was now sitting with his legs out of the door.

"Arthur Tiley." he said offering his hand. The man's grip was firm but lacked the strength that was expected in a country greeting, "Max Blake, pleased to meet ya mate, excuse the voice an' sorry I can't get up, but I aren't traveling so well these days. Me own stupid fault, bloody black horses, ya can't trust 'em ya know. Anyway enough about me. The missus, well, she's real took with that little car of yours an' she wants t' swap it for this big heap of shit that I am sitting in."

Arthur was stunned and replied, "Max I couldn't afford to pay you the difference in value of these two cars."

"We don't want no money just a straight swap."

Arthur sat on his haunches so that he was almost eye to eye with the station boss. This close he could better see that the man, was, as he had said, 'not traveling too well.' His face was pale and the left side of his head was badly scarred with only the lower part of the ear remaining. The eye on that side was milky and obviously sightless and he spoke through the right side of his mouth.

"That's a generous offer Max, but I can't accept it, your car is worth three times mine and while I would love to own a Princess, to accept your deal would be just dishonest. I'll be more than happy to give you all the information you need to purchase one, but I certainly can't swap."

John was well aware of what was going on and listened while his Dad convinced the couple that a trip to the coast would save them a lot of money and also see them with a brand new baby Austin. He was also aware that his father did this without making them feel in any way that he didn't respect their offer.

On their way back to town John asked, "Wouldn't you have liked to own their car Dad?"

"Son, I have dreamed of owning an Austin Princess and one day maybe I will but I wouldn't diddle someone to get it."

It wasn't until later in his life that John was to appreciate just what his father had done that day and that honesty was not just a matter of the price.

CHAPTER THREE

THE BREWING STORMS

It was a Saturday and John was on his way over to Ceddy's place to see if his mate was allowed to go to the river. To get there he had to go past the Council's single men's quarters; a place that was out of bounds to the Tiley brothers. Four men were sitting on the veranda having a weekend bender. John knew this, firstly by who was in the group and secondly by the beer bottles littering the area.

"G'day young Blondie!" called Les the Council grader driver.

"G'day Mr. Rosso. How ya goin'?"

"Bloody ripper, we been on the grog since knock off yesterday, but will have to steady off by tomorra cause ye old man wants us to head out real early Mondy."

Another one of the men cut into the conversation, "It's gettin' so as a bloke can't even get stuck into the grog on the weekend without worrying about the bloody boss."

"That is just rubbish, Bluey" slurred another of the drinkers.

"Don't you tell me wot's rubbish. This Council an' his old man," he said pointing at John, "Want cha t' work like a navvy, live like a black fella and then they spoil ya weekend by ya havin t' push off early Mondies"

John was not comfortable with the way the conversation was going and was desperately looking for a way to leave without being rude. "Well, I reckon I better be heading off 'çause I'm going for swim."

At this Bluey stood up, "When I was your age I could drink a bottle of grog no worries." He said taking a swig from the one in his hand. "Here have a guzzle kid show us ya gonna be a man." Waving the bottle in John's direction.

"No thanks Mister Bluey, I don't drink beer."

"Ha! Thought so you're a bloody wowser just like ya old man."

At this point the grader driver stood up. Les Rosso got to his feet. Les was a man of about forty but was someone to whom the ravages of bush life and hard living had not been kind. His body was thin and wiry, he walked with a stoop and always squinted when he spoke to anyone. He took a couple of steps in Bluey's direction, pushed his battered hat back on his head and said, "Listen ya mongrel, Arthur Tiley's a bloody good boss. He isn't a pisspot like you an' me so don't you shoot ya mouth off about him, especially not in front of young Blondie here." Bluey had about three stone and four or five inches on the grader driver and as the two men faced off, had the situation not been so serious, it looked quite comical.

John knew there was going to be trouble but was never in fear for himself, knowing full well if he had to take flight no one here, especially in their present condition, was capable of getting near him.

Bluey was the first to throw down the gauntlet, "Listen old man, go and sit down before I knock your ugly block off," he said sneering down at the older man.

At that he grabbed Rosso and literally threw him into the street quite close to where John was standing, he sat there in the dust for a few minutes as if debating any further action. Then, slowly rose and walked to the edge of the veranda, deliberately turned his back on Bluey and pulled his battered singlet over his head, he then wrapped it around his right hand, then turned around.

"Alright ya mug. If ya got the guts come an' have a go."

The younger man pulled his shirt over his head saying, "I don't want t' get any of your stinking blood on me good shirt." He then threw the shirt back onto the verandah rail and the two men started to circle each other. Bluey looked at the singlet around his adversary's hand and taunted him, "Ya frightened ya gonna hurt ya hand on me steel jaw."

"I'm gonna shut your gob good an' proper. Been wantin' to do it for a while, you big bag of shit."

The younger man rushed at Les catching him by surprise in a bear hug, with both his arms pinned by his sides and because of the difference in their heights the advantage was definitely with the bigger man. Using this advantage Bluey crashed his head into Les's face, his nose literally exploded showering both with blood. In doing this he loosened his bear hug and enabled Les to get one arm free. Whether by design or by luck it was the arm with the singlet wrapped around his fist. He immediately punched the big man directly in the face not once but a number of times and to the surprise of everyone watching, the big man's face literally came apart as each blow fell. The man screamed as one eyebrow was cut away completely revealing the bone and gristle below the surface seconds before blood gushed down his face. No ordinary blow could cause the damage done by those punches and it took a while for those watching to realise that Les Rosso had concealed the base of a broken beer bottle in the singlet he had wrapped around his hand.

The fight was over and Bluey would never look the same again. John had seen men fighting before but had never witnessed anything so cold bloodedly vicious before. The other men took Bluey inside and Les sat down on the steps his head between his hands, "Strike me pink." he muttered to no one in particular. "He was askin' for it an' I just done me bloke." With that he looked up at John, "Ya better tell your old man Blondie. I reckon he's gonna need a new drainer on our crew."

John had just turned to head home when a wild yell made him turn back around just in time to see Rosso stumble away from the veranda with a knife sticking out of his back. For a minute John was rooted to the spot in shock. Once he recovered he decided it was well and truly time to leave and, without a word took to his heels.

His father was not home when he got there but Isobel was, "Mum," he said gasping for breath, "Mister Rosso an' that Bluey bloke have had a fight an' mister Rosso hit him with a bottle in his hand."

His mother stopped the boy it mid-sentence. "Hold on John, slow down, get your breath and tell me just what happened."

The boy nodded and sat on one of the kitchen chairs, "That Bluey bloke's face was mangled an' he went an' got a knife an' stuck it into mister Rosso's back. I cleared out then so I don't know if he is dead or what."

Isobel spoke with her son as she collected the family first aid kit, "Two things, did the knife stay stuck in and was it a big knife?"

"The knife was still in his back when I left which was pretty quick, I give you the drum. The knife wasn't a real big one, a bit like the one you do the veggies with."

"OK mate, now I want you to go over to the police and get them to come over to the single men's quarters. Tell the Sergeant I will be there and the men have been on the grog."

It didn't take John long to get to the police station, once there he went straight to the Sergeant's house where his daughter Sharn was in the yard with her mother. "Excuse me Missus Hendry, is the Sarge around?"

"He is having a nap at the moment, but I can wake him if it is important."

John quickly related what had happened but made a point to add, "Me Mum has already taken off over there, but I think she was a bit worried 'cause those blokes have been on the grog all weekend."

As the local policeman's wife, Vera Hendry knew when a situation required immediate action. Leaving her daughter to look after John she went and woke her husband. Only minutes later he appeared pulling his police standard shirt over his head, "Alright young fella the missus has got a cordial and a couple of biscuits in the kitchen. When ya finish them you'd better head home. I'm on me way over to the Council. Don't you worry everything will get sorted."

Later in the evening when everybody was home Isobel told the family what had transpired. "When I got there Les was sitting on the steps drinking a beer and even though the knife was still stuck in his back it was obvious it wasn't going to kill him. Actually when I saw Bluey I was more worried about him than Les."

"Yes, from what John told me Les made a bit of mess of him with the bottom of a bottle." Her husband said. "I spoke to the other pair but they were too drunk and I couldn't get any sense out of them. The Sarge had the same problem. So tell me what happened at the hospital."

"The knife was lodged in Les's shoulder blade. Matron and I managed to get it out. She stitched him up and put him to bed. No real damage done; just a big gash where the knife initially slid down the shoulder blade."

Arthur took the tobacco packet from the table, rolled himself a cigarette, lit it then asked "What about the other bloke Bluey?"

"The flying doctor will be here tomorrow, mind you, matron did a pretty good job on most of the wounds. But the one over his eye, I don't know what they will do about it as there is no skin to cover the wound which is a good half inch wide."

"The flying doc will probably take him to the coast, they can take skin from another part of his body and put it over the wound, it's called skin grafting."

Isobel nodded knowingly. "Bluey was no Eroll Flynn before the fight and Les hasn't made any improvements that's for sure."

At this point their attention was turned to John. "What the hell were you doing at the men's quarters John?"

Their son knew this was coming and had done mental preparation. "Well," he said. "I wasn't exactly there. I was going to Ceddy's place an' mister Rosso called me over an' I just couldn't keep walking as he knew I heard him."

His father was not going to be put off that easily. "You know the quarters are off limits and no excuses." Arthur told him in no uncertain terms. Isobel also chimed in at this point, "The Sarge will want to talk to you tomorrow and he will also want to know what the damnation you were doing with a mob of drunks."

"I wasn't doing nothing with them! I was just walking past."

"Anything not nothing" his mother corrected. "And there may have been some 'walking' but there was definitely not a lot of, 'past'!" A little concerned about the involvement of the sergeant, John said, "I didn't do anything wrong. It wasn't my fault that the Bluey bloke was cranky about havin' to go out to the road camp and couldn't drink beer all day tomorra." Arthur and Isobel looked at each other and almost simultaneously asked "What on earth are you talking about?" John decided it was better to tell his parents exactly what happened. He left nothing out, including the involvement of his father's ability as 'the boss', sparking the actual fight. If the fight had not ended so seriously, both of John's parents would probably have been amused by the whole matter. Their main concern was what John had witnessed and if it had worried him. After some probing they soon realised that while the stabbing had made an impact on their son he seemed to accept that men were likely to do stupid things when they had been on the grog.

"Do ya reckon those blokes will have to go to gaol?" he asked.

His father scratched the side of his face while pondering his answer. "Hard to say son. From what the sergeant said, Bluey has a habit of using a knife so I think he could be in a bit of strife. I don't know about Les, but using a bottle on someone the way he did should see him charged with something."

John's punishment of a month with no pocket money was as painful as the belting he had fully expected. The next day after the sergeant had heard from him what had happened he said, "If I ever see you around the single men's quarters I'll kick your backside so hard your nose will bleed."

Both men were charged and as both of them pleaded guilty John was not required to appear in court. Bluey was given three months while Les was placed on probation for the same period and continued to work for the Council. After serving his time Bluey decided to try his luck in another town.

The fight and the two court cases kept the town gossips working overtime for quite a while but as it became yesterday's news, school and life for the boys returned pretty much to the way it was; except that following the pool incident, the social structure of the town had been called to account and there were other children, besides the Tileys, who no longer accepted being pushed around by the Darcies or the Doolans. Not that there was any real bullying. It was more that, by sheer numbers, these two families expected to get their own way. The exception, of course, was where either of the school's two aboriginal children were concerned.

This was brought to the fore one day before school when Maggie, the only other aboriginal child at the school wanted to play tennis. The eldest Darcy girl, Vera, said, "Boongs don't play tennis, so just piss off you stupid gin."

Maggie was only part black and a child of what was later to be called the stolen generation. Her step-parents were white and her father ran the power station. She was only in Grade Three and, because of her skin colour, did not usually attract the attention that Ceddy did. Like him Maggie kept very much to herself and was rarely seen in the playground. Yet from her reaction to what Vera said it was obvious that this was not the first time she had been picked on because of her colour.

"I can play if I want to." she replied to the surprised Vera Darcy.

"You're not allowed to play, 'cause you're a gin, so don't you get smart, just give me the racket."

Still defiant "I will not give it to you," she yelled, "And I am allowed to play."

At this Vera tried to reef the racket out of Maggie's hands, but the much smaller girl wasn't giving it up without a fight. She struggled, breaking away from Vera's grip, then rather than backing away with her prize, the child, to everyone's surprise attacked her tormentor using the racket as a club. She had hit her cowering foe three or four times before suddenly she stopped, threw the weapon on the ground and ran away crying.

The school had never had an incident like this before and it was suggested that the Head struggled to know how to deal with it. Eventually he had them come to his office, "Why did you hit Vera with the racket?" he asked Maggie whose fear of the situation was clearly visible.

The reply was barely audible, "She tried to take the racket off me and called me a gin."

"Did you do that?" he asked Vera.

"No Sir." was reply, "I just wanted to play tennis and she wasn't playing but wanted to hold the racket and that's not right is it Sir?"

To clarify the situation he called in one of other girls from the group at the courts, and when the girl confirmed what Maggie had told him he was genuinely surprised. Not because Vera had lied, he had suspected as much, but because the witness seemed unconcerned about speaking against Vera.

Both girls were punished and as there were no more than a few bruises on Vera's shoulder. Maggie's punishment was left up to her parents. For her part Vera was given extra homework: a pointless exercise as she rarely did her normal work.

The Tiley boys were pleased to have the spotlight off them for a while and a few nights later at dinner, Charles asked his parents, "Do you think girls should be punished at school the way boys are?"

His father answered, "Why do you ask this Son?" Charles told his father about the fight and suggested, "If that had been boys they would have got the cuts for sure."

Arthur told his son "Schools don't usually cane girls, but what punishment would you have given?"

Charles pondered his reply then said, "Little kids, boy or girl, shouldn't get the cane. But I reckon Vera should have got a couple of cuts, she is a bit of a bully ya know."

"But surely Maggie should not have attacked Vera with a tennis racket and should get some type of punishment for what she did?" his father suggested.

"Maybe, but because we are white I don't think we understand what it must feel like to be teased the way that Ceddy and Maggie are all the time."

At this point the debate gave way to the subject of what was for desert. However, both senior Tileys were proud of their oldest son's understanding of the problems that faced the indigenous population together with his ability to put forward his point of view.

The wet season was here again and because of it, the town and most of its population were isolated from the outside world. The heat and humidity were oppressive and the Tileys relived their arrival ten months before. Those that could afford it usually went south at this time of the year and those that couldn't put up with everybody having bouts of 'going troppo'. This well-known problem affects everyone living in the top end of Australia and can be as minor as being cranky for a few days, to committing suicide during a serious period of depression. It was common for it to be said "Don't worry about him; he's gone troppo" and it is also claimed that even animals are not immune to the affliction.

For the boys this season was exciting, with days of rain highlighted by the occasional violent storm that contained huge bolts of lightning and claps of thunder. It was also the cyclone season and the school children were given training in case any such event should occur. These exercises were taken very seriously as everyone was well aware of the destructive power of a tropical cyclone and this year their training was put to good use.

One Wednesday afternoon Arthur told the boys on his arrival home from work, "I think we might be in for a bit of a blow."

Edward looked a little worried and asked "Is it gonna be a cyclone?"

"Going to be," his mother corrected him, "And if it is we don't have to worry, the yard is clean and this is a new house; made to stand up to any cyclone." Whether Isobel believed this or not she didn't show it, and as usual the boys had blind faith in their Mother's knowledge in such matters.

The night passed without incident, but, by morning it was obvious that mother nature was going to unleash her fury. The town's school children were informed that there would be no school until the storm had passed. Just where and when it would hit nobody could predict, although there were plenty of so-called experts willing to pass an opinion, almost every conversation during that day began with "I remember back in......." and the listener was then given details of a cyclone from years gone.

Around lunch time John heard Ceddy calling to him from the back steps, "G'day mate." he said, opening the door, "What cha doin'?"

"Not much. "Came the reply "Kondie's at work with your old man an' Pollie's gone bush. She wanted me t' go with her, but she said I could stay if I came over here with you mob. She reckons our old house is gonna get flattened."

"I'll go and ask Mum but I reckon she'll be jake. What about Polly? Will she be alright in the bush if a cyclone comes?"

"She's a bush gin ya know. Kondie reckons she's knows more about the bush than he does."

"Well, OK "said John a little unsure how bush knowledge would help Polly if a cyclone was to hit the town. "Lets talk to Mum she's out the front talking to Missus Hindmarsh."

Over a cup of tea Isobel was indeed discussing the approaching blow with their neighbour from across the street. She looked around as the boys came stomping through the house, "Hello Ceddy, what do you think about getting a couple of days off school?"

"Bonza missus, but 'cause of the storm ya can't go to the creek or nothin'."

"Isobel," said the neighbor "I have to run. Thanks for the cuppa, and I will come back later and pick up that spare water container when Arthur comes home."

"No problems, I'll get John to drop it over to save you the trip."

"Mum, Polly's gone bush and Kondie wants to know if Ceddy can stay with us, 'cause their house is not as strong as this one."

Isobel turned to John's mate and asked, "Did you bring your gear with you dear because you might be here for a couple of days."

Grinning John turned to Ceddy, "See mate I told you she would be jake for you to stay, come on let's nick back to your place and grab some gear." With a nod to Isobel the boys went through the house over the back fence and walked in the direction of Ceddy's place.

"Wot will Kondie do if this cyclone comes?"

Ceddy pondered his reply, "Don't really know, but probably go to Auntie's place at the settlement."

"He can come to our place too; Mum an' Dad wouldn't mind." Ceddy shook his head, "No way mate, not that he don't like you mob but he just wouldn't stay with ya. He's funny like that."

By the time they were returning the wind was noticeably stronger with some gusts forcing the boys to brace their bodies against it. The accompanying rain stung their faces and made them turn slightly to one side, wet leaves stuck to any exposed wet skin. Ceddy laughed, "You look like yous goin' to a corroboree mate."

John grinned "I don't know about a corroboree, but I reckon this must be the cyclone 'çause its sorta blockin' out the sun. Looks like past six but I know it's a lot earlier than that. Getting' a bit spooky don't ya reckon."

By now he had to yell above the wind with Ceddy only nodding his acknowledgement. The back fence they had climbed only thirty minutes ago now quivered with the force of the wind; so much so that John indicated that they should use the side gate rather than go over as they had done earlier. Once inside, a hot drink was waiting and Isobel informed her now family of four, "Kondie and your father have had to go down to the ferry. I don't know what the problem is, but they should be back soon. The front verandah is away from the wind so let's go out there and watch the storm for a while."

The atmosphere outside had taken on an eerie yellow tinge with the rain coming in huge waves, traveling almost parallel to the ground. Trees in the school yard had already been uprooted with others almost stripped bare of their foliage.

There were very few signs of life with everyone battened down to see out the storm. "When do you reckon Dad and Kondie will be back?" an anxious Charles asked his mother. Isobel knew that her eldest son would carefully read her reply so she answered offhandedly "Oh! They will be back when they get the job done. You don't have to worry about them, they are big enough and ugly enough to look after themselves."

Ceddy was aware that his friend was anxious about his father's safety and announced "Kondie's the strongest man in the world, an' if there is any danger he would just grab your Dad and keep him safe."

The way the boy made this statement was not of bravado but simply what he believed to be true. Because of this matter of fact attitude it was easy for the three Tiley boys to accept that their father's safety was a foregone conclusion.

The sound of the storm was tremendous and the windows and doors all vibrated under the intense pressure, leaves and branches slamming into the house added to noise.

At this time a sheet of roofing iron wrapped around a power pole beside their house, "Gees where do ya reckon that come from?" John asked. Ceddy peered at the iron through the teaming rain, "It's painted so it isn't from my place." he laughed "Could be off the roof of the bottom pub: its red like that."

At this time they saw their father's ute appear out of the gloom. Because the visibility was restricting his speed the vehicle seemed to fighting its way against the might of the storm. The water being blown off the bonnet and roof gave the whole scene and elongated appearance that at times was almost ghostlike.

As the boys watched, another sheet of roofing iron slammed into the fence and in an instant a section of it was ripped out of the ground.

Safely in the house Arthur called the family together. "Firstly Ceddy, Kondie is up at the settlement where he feels he might be needed and says you are to stay here with us.

All you kids are to get the single mattresses off the beds and put them in the bathroom, fill the bathtub with water and any containers we have in the kitchen. Once you have done this grab all the tinned food and put it in the bathroom as well."

"Did the Council get any news about how strong or how long this storm will be?" asked his wife.

"All the council knows is what came through on the Flying Doctor radio and that was that it was a cyclone and we could expect it to come across the coast around here." was the reply.

Outside the wind tore at the small town, hurtling anything not tied down into oblivion. The boys watched as the side section of the school roof was peeled off.

The boys watched as the side section of the school roof was peeled off. The house creaked and groaned and water poured in around any windows or doors facing the storm but it stood firm. Then, in an instant, the wind dropped and an eerie calm descended. Charles was the first to speak "Wow! I'm glad that is over - didn't it stop quickly?"

"Sorry to disappoint you Son." his father told him, "We are now in the eye of the cyclone. In a few minutes the wind will start again but it will be coming from the other side. He quickly went on to explain the circular action of the storm that rotated around the centre or eye.

True to their father's prediction, within ten minutes the wind began again. However, this time it was almost instantly at gale force with no lead-in as had been the case when the storm approached originally. For another two hours the cyclone battered the house, the front double doors blew in and the window in the kitchen blew out, but other than that they came through unscathed. The power wasn't restored for three days; the school roof was the main casualty and was covered by a tarpaulin until the end of the school year.

The morning after the storm John went with his friend to inspect his house "D'ya reckon Polly will be back?"

"Soon as she thinks it's safe she'll be back" replied his mate.

The house was still intact and smoke was drifting from the chimney "I told ya she's back already!" Still chatting the boys clattered through the kitchen but it was Kondie who met them and not Polly.

"Where's Auntie?" Ceddy asked immediately.

"Still in the bush, I reckon." came the reply, but the big man's actions clearly showed that he was concerned.

"Maybe me an' John could go an' take a gander."

"She would go up behind the hospital. She got a special place up there somewhere if ya wanna go take a look."

"What d' ya reckon mate?" he asked his friend. John didn't give it a second thought, "We better tell Mum where we are goin', but we can grab a sanga an' a bottle of water to take with us 'cause Missus Polly might want a bit of a feed."

The boys returned to the Tileys' house explaining to Isobel what they proposed. "I think that is a good idea boy, but if Polly has had an accident or is crook, one of you stay with her and the other go and get the sister from the hospital, is that clear?" Both the boys agreed to the conditions laid down, packed a bit of food either for themselves or Polly, if they found her and she was in need. They both knew the bush in the area that Kondie had suggested they look and it wasn't long before Ceddy called to his friend, "Somebody done a bit a cookin' here not too long ago. But I don't reckon it was Polly."

John came into the clearing where Ceddy was carefully examining the ground around what was a recent camp fire. "What cha found mate?"

"Well this fire was lit before the sun come up, but this was a black fella not Polly. Foot's too big an' from his walk I reckon it'll be old Jimmy. He gorn off towards the settlement but maybe he seen Aunty."

"Ah! Your pullin' me leg, how do ya know it's Mister Jimmy?"

Ceddy seemed a little surprised that his friend would doubt him. "Old Jimmy he got a toe that got broke long time back, an' it sorta sticks out a bit. You look here at this footprint: see this toe here he sticks out, an' when this fella walks he take one step a bit shorter than the other. Only one bloke I know got a funny foot an' walk like that: Ole Jimmy."

It was only after looking two or three times that John was able to distinguish the signs that his mate had pointed out and was amazed that Ceddy was able to pick up these with what appeared to be a glance. "Gee mate, you make me look like a complete dunce with your bush stuff. I reckon you could track a snake on a rock."

Ceddy shook his head. "Nah, I just look for easy signs. Kondie he can see signs that aren't there an' Auntie's pretty good too. That's why we don't have to worry too much about her. 'Cept she gettin' pretty old and maybe fell over an' got hurt, but let's find Ole Jimmy t' see what he got to say."

The settlement was a bit of a mess with most of the makeshift humpies blown to pieces and spread into the surrounding scrub. Nobody seemed too worried about the loss of accommodation, with small groups sitting around fires all with food or a billy in the ashes. The boys chatted to their friends for a while before going down to the river where they found Jimmy.

Ceddy addressed the old man, "Uncle Jimmy, we lookin' for Aunty Polly an' wonderin' if maybe you seen her up in the scrub?"

Jimmy scratched his chin replying, "Boy! You think I walk around with me eyes closed? I seen her when that ol' storm blowin' like God just open the door. She come along to me camp an' we had a cuppa just after it was settled down. You don't have to worry nothing 'bout that bush gin: she plenty bush smart dat ol' girl."

Ceddy thought for a while before replying, "But I seen all your signs an' if Aunty was there I wudda seen her signs as well."

Old Jimmy smiled "She your Aunty boy. You should know if she don't want to leave no signs then she don't leave no signs." Ceddy did not seem surprised by this answer and nodded. "I forget what she kin do when she want to."

Walking back to the settlement a puzzled John asked "What was all that about? I know I am not much good at looking for signs but you're a ripper an' I reckon if she was at Mister Jimmies camp you would have seen something."

Ceddy shook he head. "You a white fella an' you don't understand that people like Aunty are different. If she don't want to leave no mark then she has the power to do that." John didn't understand any of what his friend was saying but guessed it was one of those things that you just had to accept.

The boys looked around for a bit longer then decided to head back to town, pretty sure now that Aunty Polly was OK. "D' ya think we should ask if anybody wants a hand before we leave?" John asked.

Ceddy shook his head. "Nobody doin' nuffin' just now. Black fella way is just eat a bit of tucker, drink some tea an' have a smoke. But most we talk, this our way of makin' sure that nobody still shakin' from the storm. If they is, then a bit of a yarn make em feel good, an' they not shakin' no more."

Polly turned up later that afternoon none the worst for the experience. John did ask her what it was like in the bush when the cyclone came, she explained in halting English, "Dat bush belong t' ma people an' she not gonna do nuttin 't me."

Much to the boys' disappointment no school was missed as a result of the storm damage and after only a short time the storm was forgotten and, bar a few scars, the town was back to normal. The school year only had a few weeks to run and already Charles had taken his high school entrance exam or scholarship as it was called in those days. This tested the children in three subjects - Maths, English and Social Studies. It was state run and the results were printed in the paper for all to see.

The end of year sports were in full swing with an event almost every afternoon with the boys all doing well in their age groups. After much cajoling from the Tileys, Ceddy decided to compete for the first time and he was the one who excelled, winning every event in his age group.

As could be expected, this winning streak was not taken well in all quarters and Ceddy was rarely seen after they left the school yard. However, he was determined to put the Darcy and Doolan kids in their place on the sports field as often as he could. He knew full well that being beaten by a Boong was an experience they were not happy about.

It was the Saturday before school was to break up and the Tiley boys had just received their pocket money for the week. "I'm gonna grab Ceddy an' get a big bottle of Cherry Cheer. That's just what I feel like." said John. To his surprise his older brother replied "Good idea. Edward and I will head down and meet you at the shop."

John headed off to see if Ceddy was home, he knocked on the verandah post and called out, "Are you there mate?"

Pollies voice came from the back "He's in the dunny. Come in." John went through the house to the back yard, "G'day Missus Polly; how are ya?"

"I'm real good. Had a crook back but a coupla nights in the bush sorted 'er right out. Your mob good?"

"Yeh, we are all great thanks. Can Ceddy come to the shop?"

"Up to him; that boy do what he want."

The dunny door made a bang as Ceddy emerged. "Thought I could hear your voice mate. How's it goin'?" he asked, washing his hands under the tap in the rainwater tank.

"Great. We're all going to the shop; you wanna come?"

"I reckon but Kondie didn't give me my pocket money yet." Turning to Polly, he asked, "Kin you give me two bob Aunty?"

Making a show of muttering and complaining Polly got her battered old red purse from the kitchen. "Now, I want this back when Kondie gives you some money.".

Ceddy gave a cheeky grin and said "You bet Aunty. Thanks a lot."

The boys all met outside the store and went in together. "G'day you lot. Pocket money day is it?"

Charles spoke for the group "Hello Mister Daws. Yep, we reckon school's as good as over for the year so we are going to have a bit of a party. We got enough for three big bottles of soft drink, four sherbet bags, a fruit and nut chocolate and one and six pence worth of raspberries."

The shop keeper looked surprised "You blokes rob a bank did ya?"

"We got the money" said John, adding "We brought three old bottles as well."

"Good on ya so. What soft drink do you want?"

Here the youngest member of the group spoke up "Cherry Cheer, lemonade and a bottle of Sars please."

"Well you certainly had that worked out didn't ya. Only three bottles and four kids, how's that going to work? Do you want some paper cups?"

"Nah thanks. We just hand em around, so everybody gets some of all the different drinks. Ya just wipe the bottle on ya shirt an' she's right." John informed the little man on the other side of the counter.

The Daws family had owned the town store for three generations but, sadly, Peter was to be the last, as his marriage to Mary had never been blessed with children. The store itself was a reflection of the couple: small, but very neat and tidy with a place for everything and everything in its place. Both of them were born and bred locals but unlike most they kept to themselves and, while they received all the town gossip, were renowned for never passing it on.

They knew all the children of the town especially well: it is said that Peter kept a book that listed what each child had stolen from the store: some goods he had recovered on the spot and some he had not. Parents were rarely informed of these offences but the local police sergeant was occasionally asked to speak to repeat offenders that had been caught in the act. As the store was by no means the Daws' only source of income, the people of the town were able to put things on tick until their circumstances improved; a facility that was rarely abused and much appreciated, thereby adding to the couples' standing in the community.

The boys gave a cheery wave as they left "Thanks Mister Daws see ya later. Is it ok if we sit outside?"

"Go for your life boys, if you want. Grab a couple of fruit crates as well."

"She'll be right; we can sit in the gutter."

The boys sat down, took the caps off the bottles using John's pocket knife and cut the chocolate into four equal pieces. Happily munching and passing the drinks around they didn't notice the Doolan and Darcy boys walk up behind them. As they arrived Jack said "Look at the Boong lovers sharing a bottle with their black mate. What ya drinkin'? Metho and boot polish?"

Quickly whacking the caps back on the bottles and stashing them against the wall of the shop, the four shoved the remains of their feast into various pockets. Not particularly worried by the fact that they were outnumbered and out-sized, the challenge was taken. "I'd rather have a black for a mate then one of you web fingered spaso's." said John.

"Who are you callin' a spaso? My mum reckons you Tileys are just blow-ins." one of the Doolans in John's class said.

"What's a blow-in?" he was asked.

"Er, I don't know but that's what she said."

Ray, the oldest of Darcy boys, was standing next to Jack and spoke for the first time, "Look at your mate the Boong, hiding away and letting you stand up for him."

He was right in a way. Ceddy and Edward had taken a position a couple of yards away.

As if on cue Edward joined his two brothers and stood between them. Jack poked a finger in his direction, "What's the midget going to do?" he said with an attempt at a laugh.

Charles pushed the hand aside saying "You're big at picking on smaller kids aren't ya Jack? If ya want a blue, what about just you and me or you and my younger brother John?"

Jack was a little surprised at this direct attack on him and before he could speak John added "You lot are a mob of dingo's. You're nearly four years older than me but I still reckon I could flatten ya." At this point Jack gave the youngest Tiley a shove as if clearing a space for him and John to do battle. Edward's reaction surprised everyone, he swung his clenched fist and smacked Ray Darcy just below his left eye. The skin split like a water melon which was not surprising seeing he held a fist sized rock in his hand, blood went everywhere, the Darcy and Doolan kids quickly retreated to the other side of the road from where the two sides traded insults.

A rock ricocheted off the corrugated iron side of the store followed by two or three that fell short. By now the Tiley boys had collected some ammunition themselves and returned fire. The storekeeper joined in the fray shouting from the relative safety of the store, "Stop this immediately! Stop it or I am calling the police." A misdirected throw actually hit one of the front windows - luckily without breaking it. "OK! That's it I am going to call the Sergeant." was shouted from within.

The Tileys, for their part, were too busy dodging and returning fire to pay much heed to the calls to cease fire. The battle was not going well and both Charles and John had been hit at least once. "I reckon we'd better quit before Edward cops one." said Charles "There are five of them and as Ceddy won't help we're in trouble."

He was right, Ceddy stood at the side of the shop and had not involved himself in the stone throwing. John was not at all surprised at his friend's lack of involvement, knowing full well his fear of the establishment and commented "Ceddy is frightened of gettin' into trouble an' being sent away." Looking at his friend he continued "It's OK mate, we understand but we all better get ready to make a run 'cause we are just gettin' clobbered."

At that moment, the shy aboriginal boy decided he had taken enough to last a lifetime. He carefully selected four or five stones and stood between his two mates.

"Hey Jack!" he shouted "This one is for you!"

Now, throwing is a natural art for aboriginals as in times not long passed their very existence depended on this ability. Ceddy was no exception and on many occasions John had marveled at the remarkable power and accuracy that his slightly built friend had. The first stone did not miss and Jack fell to the ground holding his hip in pain, the second and third throws also found their mark and, as if by magic, the battle was over. "Hell cobber, that was fantastic! Ole Jack will be walking with a limp for a few days. This will go well with Ray's sore head." John said, clapping his friend on the back. Meanwhile Charles had walked across the road to find out what damage Ceddy's three throws had done, "You alright Jack?" he asked.

"Bloody hell! That little Boong can throw can't he."

"Sure can!" Charles replied. "That's why he should be in the school cricket team."

At this time the police Land Rover arrived, the Sergeant got out and came over to where Jack and Charles were talking. "What the hell do you kids think you're doing, having a rock fight in front of the store? I should take you all down to the goal and lock you up for the night. Tiley you get over there with your brothers. I'll have a word to you lot in a minute." Charles went back to the others to find John comforting Ceddy who was almost throwing up from fear. "Ceddy's frightened that he will get sent away to some island where bad aboriginals get sent." he told Charles.

Charles thought for a bit and said "You just watched. We were hoping you would join in but ya didn't, OK?".

Ceddy nodded in agreement and stepped back into the shadow of the store. After a few minutes the Sergeant came back to their side of the street, "No one there knows who started the fight or who threw what, so you lot had better tell me."

As was normal for the brothers, Charles did the talking "It was just sort of push and shove Sir, but then we started throwing rocks."

"I accept that but who smacked Ray in the eye?"

Edward found his voice and stammered, "I did Sir. He said some bad things but I meant to hit Jack, because he was going to fight John and he's a lot bigger and older than him Sir but I sorta missed Sir."

The bush policeman muttered to himself "No wonder that big lug kept quiet about who busted Ray's eye." Then asking "And who did all the damage in the throwing war; again, that lot didn't know." John stepped forward. "Musta been Charles or me Sir, as Edward can't throw that far and Ceddy stayed out of it."

He was a typical country copper who relied on his gut feeling and common sense to sort out most problems, he looked over at Ceddy and said "You'd better hop it then young Ceddy. Go on! Get off home."

Ceddy swallowed took a deep breath and stepped out of the shadows. He stood to attention with his hands behind his back, "I did throw some rocks Mister Policeman. Charles an' John are me mates an stickin' up for me; but I gotta be a mate to them too."

The Sergeant shook his head "Did I ask you to talk lad?"

"No Sir."

"And what did I tell you to do?"

"To get off home Sir, but I have to tell you..." before he could say any more the Sergeant interrupted him, "I didn't ask you to tell me anything. Just do as you are told and take off, now!"

Ceddy looked at John, whose eyes immediately told him that not only was it OK for him to go, but it was what they, including the policeman, wanted. His face showed relief as he said, "Well I reckon I'll be off home. See ya all later."

"We didn't finish our party so take the Sarse an' I'll see ya tomorra." John said to the quickly retreating back.

The sergeant turned to the boys "I hope you lot realise just how serious this battle today could have been. As it is, nobody got badly hurt and nothing got broken so you were all lucky. I will drop by and have a word with your old man so you can warn him that I'll be around."

Charles asked cautiously, "Er, Ceddy's not in strife is he Sir?"

The reply was a relief but not what the boys expected. "I know exactly what happened here today and while I will not tolerate this type of thing, I do know what that boy puts up with day after day. I also know how you blokes stick up for him and one day this state will wake up to itself; and thank God for people like you and your Mum and Dad. You lot don't have to worry about Ceddy as far as I am concerned. Now, get yourselves off home."

The boys didn't need to be told a second time but as they left, without a word, Edward walked to the policeman and stuck out his hand. The big man took it, shook it then ruffled the youngest Tiley's hair saying "No more rocks OK?" Edward grinned, nodded his head and joined his brothers.

The battle of Bourke Street as the incident became known, was big news in the small town; not so much because of what happened, but the fact someone had taken on the Doolans and Darcys.

With the school year about to draw to a close, it was obvious to the community that with three of the oldest Darcy and Doolan children not to be at school the following year, the place would definitely change for the better. Nobody expected the lot of the two indigenous pupils to improve, but they realised that change was in the air and maybe, just maybe, the battle of Bourke Street had not just been a bunch of kids throwing rocks but a town starting to grow up.

CHAPTER FOUR

'NO SWEET SORROW'

Christmas came and went and the new school year started. A week prior to the start of term Charles left for high school.

John had never been parted from his brother before and was finding it difficult to come to terms with the empty place at the table at meal times. While the three brothers never lived in each other's pockets, they were always there to look out for each other and, with Charles's departure, John felt a huge responsibility for his younger brother's wellbeing.

"Do ya reckon Charles will make a lot of friends at his new high school?" he asked his mother one afternoon.

"I am sure he will, dear. We received a letter from your grandmother and she enclosed this piece out of the newspaper". At that she handed him a clipping from a paper called *The Advocate*.

The heading read "State's Youngest Is Our School's One Hundredth Pupil. The article told of a bush lad having to get special permission, because of his age, to go to high school. It gave a little of the family background and that he also took the school enrolment number to one hundred for the first time.

"Does this mean there are a hundred kids at Charles's school?"

His mother smiled at her son's voice, "Yes. I think they finished up with about one hundred and twenty."

"A hundred and twenty kids at one school." said John in amazement "He'll get some mates from that many kids. Will I have to go to a school as big as that when I do scholarship?"

"I guess you will. They don't have small high schools like the primary ones you have been to. But, by the time you are ready we should have moved to a town that has a school you can go to."

"Will Ceddy go away to high school when he does scholarship?"

"I don't know Son. I would like to think he will, but to be honest he doesn't have the same chance as most white kids do."

"Why doesn't Ceddy join our family and then you and Dad could make sure he got as much chance as white kids."

"It's not so easy John. Dad and I have spoken to Kondie and the authorities but we are not in a position to do anything, mainly because we haven't known Ceddy very long and we move around a lot."

"But they should ask Ceddy. I reckon he would think it was a good idea."

"There is a lot more than you could understand, especially with this Kondie thing."

"What's the matter with Kondie is he sick or something?"

"No he is not sick." Isobel said, continuing, "You remember the other night when Dad had to go out with the sergeant?"

"Yep! It was last Thursday."

Isobel nodded her agreement, "Well Dad went to see Kondie because he had gone to the pub and got into trouble. The police wanted to take him to the goal but you know how big and strong he is.

"Ceddy reckons he is the strongest man in the country."

"I don't know about that but he was certainly too strong for the two policemen to put him into the police truck. That's why they came to get Dad, because they hoped he could calm Kondie down and get him to go with them."

"But Ceddy told me that if they got into trouble they would get sent away to an island for bad Aboriginals so Kondie wouldn't do anything bad would he?"

"Well, we don't think he did anything bad, but he drank too much beer and then he went to the pub to get some more, they wouldn't sell it to him so he got angry. The police came but when they tried to take him away he just hung onto the bar rail and was too strong for the police to move."

"So did they come and get Dad 'cause he's pretty strong?"

Isobel laughed. "No, they got your father because he is Kondie's boss and friend."

"But a lot of people on the Council get drunk and fight. Remember Mister Rosser, you said the other bloke looked like he got hit by a bus. The police didn't come and get Dad when that happened."

The boy's mother thought carefully about her reply. "The trouble with the laws at the moment is that they are a bit one-sided when it comes to Aborigines. The reason Kondie can live in town is because he is sort of in between. This is a bit like a special deal for him because he a good bloke but if he gets into trouble the government can take this privilege away from him."

"That seems very unfair. Just because he is black he has to be better than anyone who is white."

"Sadly, that is the way the law is at the moment and the only thing we can do is vote to get the law changed."

"Can we vote so Kondie doesn't get sent away?"

Again Isobel brooded over her answer. "The law takes a long time to change son. Kondie will have to go to court and then they will decide on his punishment. This is the reason Ceddy hasn't been around for the last few days. He and Aunty Polly have gone up to the settlement until this Kondie thing is sorted out."

"He told me he was going to visit some relations, but he didn't say anything about Kondie being in strife."

In the days to follow the boys found themselves wanting to defend their friend against the taunts of the other kids at school but yet not fully understanding what the whole business was about. Their Mother had warned them that they could expect some rough treatment because of their friendship with the Polly family and, while wanting to lash out, both had kept their feelings in check and the week at school had passed without incident. In fact by Friday the whole thing had almost played itself out but of course Ceddy had not yet returned to school and John knew that they would be tested when this happened.

The school teachers were also aware of the problems and perhaps wisely decided to let the children sort things out. They knew the physical risk was small as Ceddy was well versed in avoiding danger and of course there was the Tiley factor. They had the boy return for his first day on a Friday: a clever move as, while they could see the hurt Ceddy felt from the cruel taunts thrown at him, they hoped that the weekend would serve as a gap and the issue would just die on its own as it had initially. This proved to be the case, helped of course by the absence of the older children who had not returned at the start of the school year. John was still confused about the process of the law and this was made worse when he went to his mate's place on the Saturday after his return to school. He knocked on the veranda floor and yelled "Are ya at home mate?". To his surprise Kondie replied. "He's gorn t' the shop, but you can come an' wait; I reckon he be back pretty damn soon." John entered to find the big man sittting in his favorite beaten old stuffed chair, "G'day Mr. Kondie." he said, a little stuck for words, "I er, didn't know you were er, home."

Seeing the boy was confused he explained, "Your old man put up the fifty quid for me bail so, until I go to court, I kin go back t' work an' do what I want except I can't go to anudder place. If I go walkabout y' Dad will do his fifty quid so I just gotta stay an' face the Magistrate."

"I reckon it must be tough not to be white. My Mum said we gotta vote to make things the same for you blokes."

"This is my country ya know Blondie. My people bin here fer thousands of years. We don't mind to share, but there should be some respect. Dis is a big place, plenty of room for black and white, but I don't think us black fellas should have to ask permission to do our stuff."

"What do you think will happen when ya go to court? An' what about Ceddy; is he gonna be OK?"

"Don't know. White fellas' laws are pretty heavy on us blacks. Maybe I go to jail maybe not. If I go to island jail Ceddy and Polly kin come with me but if udder jail then I reckon they have to go back up onto our country settlement; this is where Ceddy were born an' he know dat place."

John listened intently watching Kondie's face tell of his sadness at the prospect of being separated from his family. He had never had a conversation of more than a few words with the big man prior to this and was proud to be accepted as someone mature enough to understand the pain he was feeling.

"My Mum and Dad are pretty angry ya know. I think we'll be movin' again soon. Us kids know when Dad's not happy an' that means packin' up and hittin' the road."

"Why would ya leave? Your old man does a good job an', 'cept for a couple of blokes on the Council, he gets on good with everyone."

"I don't know why, but when Mum and Dad get a bit of agro they just pack up an' we shove off to somewhere else. They always tell us to sort things out, but it must be different for grown-ups."

"Your Dad is a pretty smart fella so you just follow him an' you'll be jake."

Over the next month John often thought about what Kondie had said and while the boys were never concerned about moving, and usually they were not aware of any of the politics around the move, this time they were, which somehow made it more personal; a feeling that did not sit well, especially with John.

One afternoon after school their Mother announced that Ceddy was going to be staying with them for a couple of weeks. "The magistrate has withdrawn Kondie's bail." she told the boys. "Because Polly has gone walkabout, Ceddy would be on his own so he is going to stay with us."

John was excited at the prospect of his friend staying and asked, "Do ya reckon he might stay with us for good?"

His mother shook her head "No dear, there is no chance of that, and I have already explained why."

"I know, but I thought maybe the government had been thinking twice."

Isobel laughed "You mean having second thoughts and I am not sure this government is much in the thinking department, once or twice."

Not sure what his mother meant John let that subject drop but asked, "Why are some people white and some black? 'Cause if everyone was sorta brown then there would be none of this pickin' on people stuff."

Again his mother laughed, "I'm not sure that is the answer, but hopefully in time we will better understand and accept cultures that are different from our own."

At this moment Ceddy appeared at the back door, "Giday. Mister Tiley come t' my place an' he said to get some of me gear an' come over here. I dunno why but he said you would explain Missus."

Isobel shook her head muttering, "Typical bloody man!" then to Ceddy, "Come in mate, you want a Milo?"

"No thanks Missus I just want to know what is goin' on. Kondie wasn't home so he couldn't tell me nothin'."

Isobel asked her sons to leave her for a while and got the boy to take a seat.

Later John and Ceddy were sitting on the back steps. It was a balmy evening and both were a lot quieter than usual, eventually John asked, "Wot ya reckon is gonna happen?"

"I dunno mate, I've never been away from Kondie an' Polly before. But your mum said I kin stay with you mob until things get sorted out."

John nodded, indicating he already knew what had been said between Ceddy and his mother. "Don't you worry," he said putting his arm around his friend's shoulders, "Mum an' Dad 'll make sure everything will be jake. They are grouse when ya think things are real crook, us kids found some bombs once and didn't tell anybody, some people go to jail in New Guinea for keeping bombs and stuff but we just got a good talking to from an army bloke."

"You mean bombs like ya see in the pictures coming out of planes?"

"Yep, but these were sorta small ones and in New Guinea people were always finding war things." As he spoke to his mate his mind went back to the bomb incident and even though more then two years had passed it was still very clear in his mind. Most probably because of the realization of what could have been, brought home in no uncertain fashion by both their parents together with an army bomb disposal officer.

"Ya mean ya actually got a real one?"

"We found a bunch but only took a couple of 'em home."

"Aw! You musta really copped it when ya turned up at home with a couple a bombs."

"Fair go mate, we weren't crazy enough t' show 'em to Mum and Dad."

"What a ripper! Ya gotta tell me what happened."

"I'll tell ya but don't say anything to Mum or Dad as they still get cranky if we ever talk about it."

John related to his friend the story of the boys' very serious flirtation with death.

We were no different from any children our age in those days, I reckon, because it was not long after the end of World War Two; us livin' in New Guinea was fantastic, sorta like havin' an adventure in your own book.

We lived at the 'Six Mile', a small place with a few houses, a shop an' garage; because of its name I reckon we were six miles from town. It was near the Port Moresby airport and this was the place where a lot stuff went on during the war and especially when it was nearly over. A lot of people were around there and they reckon that was the base that pushed the Japs all the way back to where they came from. I tell ya the place was littered with all kinds of wrecks and we played war in real army trenches. Our cubby house was one of those cement rooms underground where they use to keep all the stores of bullets an' things. We played in old planes that still had their guns and some had lotsa holes in 'em from being shot at.

At the first house we lived in we found two boxes with a long belt of little pockets with bullets in them; they looked like a string of huge fire crackers, we gave 'em to Dad and he took 'em to the army. But the Six Mile house was better, an' it wasn't made out of paper like the first place. Most afternoons after school, we went exploring and on one of these days we were checking out these mounds of dirt, sorta made into the shape of a horse shoe. We knew that the pilots used these for bombing practise an' Charles thought we might find some bomb bits. But boy! I tell ya mate, in one of them we found better than bits, no bull! Laying in the bottom of one of the horseshoe things was a bunch of real bombs. They weren't huge big ones 'cause I could just pick one up. It looked like someone was collecting them up, 'cause they were laid out neat and tidy in a line and had numbers on 'em.

We thought it would be a ripper if we could get a couple before they got taken away: we guessed whoever stacked em up must be coming back. Of course we had been to the army talks at school about how dangerous all this unexploded or unfired war time stuff was, but we reckoned if these bombs didn't explode when they hit the ground after being dropped from a plane, then they weren't gonna blow up. So we got a piece of wire from a fence put it through the fins of three of the bombs an' were gonna drag 'm home. But it was too heavy for us to drag three so we decided 't only take two, this was pretty easy as two together slid along the ground no worries.

Once we had our bombs home we stashed them under the back veranda where not even the house boi went. We were still a bit worried about taking the bombs so we reckoned we better not go to the horseshoe place for a while. Charles thought because they had numbers on them, somebody would know some were missing. We didn't think we had stole them because everybody picked up war stuff. We all played with the ones at home, pretended the veranda was a plane and chucked 'm over the rail; ya know we even tried t' take one apart with a big pipe spanner.

One afternoon Charles decided to revisit the dirt horseshoe to check what had happened to the bombs we left: if they were gone or anything. He took Edward and our house boi's son Peepee, funny name eh, Peepee. On their way they walked past a couple of soldiers sittin' in a jeep. I'm not sure they exactly walked past them, maybe sorta around and up the hill a bit. They were gettin' near to the bank of the horseshoe, an' lucky for them they were comin' from behind 'cause that was when the bombs went off.

I was walking down the road to our house when they went off. Holy mackerel! It was loud an' when I'd seen this huge cloud of dust I knew immediately what had happened and was a bit worried 'cause I thought Charles or Edward might have set 'em off. A cuppla minutes later Peepee came running out of the bush, his only words to me as he ran past was 'big boom big boom', Edward wasn't far behind and soon Charles came out too. I tell ya mate they looked pretty funny all covered with dirt, leaves an' sticks.

Charles was telling me what had happened when this army jeep with three soldiers in it came screaming up. The boss was one of 'em and he leapt out and shouted at Charles wanting to know what the children were doing there. Charles told him they were just goin' for a walk, an' I reckon this officer, boss bloke knew his men messed up and should have stopped anyone from goin' down the track. I tell ya cobber, I nearly dropped me duds when them bombs when off. Charles an' Edward were even worse; ya know, they couldn't hear properly for a couple of days, so we reckoned we better tell the soldier blokes about our bombs.

Strike me pink, the boss officer nearly had a fit when Charles told him. He said to the others that he told them he hadn't made a mistake with the number of bombs. He was damn cranky I can tell ya, he shouted at a couple of the blokes t' move all the people in the nearby houses away. Anyone livin' near us had t' go up the road, I had to go too, but as we had the bombs hidden under the house, Charles had to go with two soldiers, all dressed in gear that made 'em look like they were from outer space, an' show them where we had the bombs under some old wood and garden stuff.

When everyone was up the road a bit they took a couple of box things in, then they musta put bombs in these 'cause when they came out the boxes were put in the jeep an' driven slow and carefully back down the track to where we got 'em from. A bit later they let 'em off, not as big a bang as the first one but pretty big anyway. Our luck ran out even more because Mum and Dad came home just before they let off our bombs, an' if ya reckon the bombs made a noise you shudda heard the old man go off. We had told 'em everything before the soldiers came back and the old man give the officer a rip for not having a proper guard when they let off the bombs. He was also pretty cranky that they had left the things after they knew where they were, ya know, even though it sounded like he blamed the army blokes but when they were gone, boy, did we cop it!

The army bloke came to our school a couple of days later and gave every one a big talk. He got Charles t' tell everyone what it was like to be close to a bomb goin' off an how lucky we were not to have been blown up."

Ceddy wasn't sure if his mate was pulling his leg and asked, "Did ya ever find any more bombs?"

"Nah, we got the shell of a big one but it was empty. Dad found a hand grenade when he was building a new road. He took it to the police but they made him take it to the army. He saw the bloke who came to our place and found out he was the senior bloke of the mob that goes around blowing up old war stuff."

"Gees mate it musta been great livin' at that place. What were the people there like?"

"They talk a different way to us 'an they're black with really curly hair but other than that they are the same as us."

"So if they are black they could be rellies of mine, don't ya think?"

"I'm not sure 'bout that, they were black but didn't look nothin' like you cobber."

Changing the subject John asked, "Are you scared about what's gonna happen with all this stuff with Kondie?"

"Yea, I am a bit, but us black fellas have got lotsa aunties an' uncles so if the worst happens I could go back to me mum or another aunty. I don't want to leave Kondie, 'cause he's not like the rest of my mob. He makes me do things, an' I know its because he wants me to grow up to be a good person. He reckons being a good person is the main thing an' going t' school is number two."

The boys were called to dinner and John never found out what his mate would have preferred to do, but, two days later, the choice was taken out of his hands. Kondie was found guilty and sentenced to two years on Coco Island a prison farm established for aboriginals where it was possible for the prisoners to have their families with them. The whole thing happened very quickly. Kondie was taken away immediately after his court appearance and his family was given one week to follow him or they would lose the automatic right to follow. If this happened, those designated as his family would then have to apply to the court for permission to follow. As if by magic Polly reappeared and Ceddy spent the remaining days with her at the settlement. Their meager belongings took very little packing and while the boy never returned to school he was at the Tiley's every afternoon when the brothers came home.

The day before Ceddy left, he and John decided to go to the river for the last time together. John got his pocket money early that week and decided to buy a bottle of soft drink on their way. "G'day! Mister Dawes, kin I have a big bottle of Cherry Cheer please? Me and Ceddy are goin' t' the river 'cause tomorra he's going to the island place where Kondie is, so I reckon I won't see him no more."

"That is a bit rough, son." the understanding shop keeper said. "I tell you what, you buy a bottle of drink and I'll give you a packet of iced vo-vo's to have a bit of a feed as well as a last drink together."

At this point Ceddy spoke. "I hope I kin get Cherry Cheer at this place where Kondie is." then added, "You are a pretty good bloke Mister Dawes an' thanks for the biscuits; me an' John will slip into them I kin tell ya."

A bit taken back he replied, "Kondie got a rough deal son, an' a lot of people in this town should be ashamed of the whole business. He's a bloody good bloke your uncle an' if you grow up to be half the man he is you'll be right."

At the river the boys ate and drank until finally Ceddy broke the silence. "I kin write ya a letter t' tell ya what this new place is like. I've never written a letter but it would be good because mates an' brothers should know what the other fella is doin' don't cha reckon."

John pondered for a few minutes hit by the reality that tomorrow his mate would be leaving his life. During his short life he had started anew many times, but he had always been the one leaving so this was breaking new ground for the boy.

"I tell ya, for me, once a mate always a mate. It would be grouse if we wrote to each other, but I reckon when we grow up we'll still be mates an' knock around together again."

They decided to take the old corrugated iron canoe for one last paddle. It leaked as badly as ever but for once neither of them bothered to bail the water out and as they neared the shore on their return the noble craft sank. Maybe this was a symbolic end to a relationship, that had stood up against the prejudice of a town, had made them better people and had given both boys a wonderful understanding of each other's culture.

The next day Isobel packed the clothes Ceddy had at the Tiley's then took him and her two sons to his house, there Polly was already packed and ready to go. The police sergeant met them all at the airport and gave Polly an envelope containing tickets and travel expenses. He then said, "I am sorry about everything and want you to know it was not my decision to have Kondie charged. He is a fine man and you, Ceddy, should be proud of him." With that he nodded to Isobel and returned to his vehicle.

Soon the ageing DC3 arrived and while the luggage was loaded John and Ceddy went to the rain water tank at the side of the building. John cupped his hand under the tap turned it on and drank, after him his friend did likewise. "I don't wanna go on that 'plane. What keeps it in the air?"

"The engines do that. The wings don't flap like a bird ya know. We went to New Guinea in a plane like this an' it was jake mate; ya don't have t' worry."

As they walked back to the gate John put his hand on his mate's shoulder in a child's way of acknowledging his friend's pain. The passengers were called and Isobel walked to the 'plane with Polly explaining the process of boarding.

Ceddy shook hands with Edward then turned to John, "We'll see each other again OK." he said as he took his friend's hand between his two.

John nodded, the boys briefly locked eyes then Ceddy turned and walked to the aircraft.

At the bottom of the steps he hugged Isobel goodbye and at the top he turned and waved to the boys, then disappeared inside. The two weeks following Ceddy's departure were tough on John and Edward. By and large at school they were pretty well left alone: a few smart comments were met with a death stare from John that made anyone think twice about continuing. Even the teachers were able to recognise that the boys should be given a little bit of leeway over this period; however it was obvious that the brothers blamed the town for the departure of their friend.

About two months after Ceddy left the boys came home from school to find their father was home from work early. John met him with a grin and, "G'day Dad. Crikey, you're home early, are we gonna go out to a job or something?"

"No, that's not the reason, I'm home early because a couple of weeks ago I applied for a job with another shire about two days' drive from here and today they called me to say I had the job if I want it." John was puzzled. His father had never discussed a proposed move in this way before.

"Are we going to move then," he asked.

"Well, it's a great job," his father continued, "But Mum and I want to hear what you two think. We know you have been happy here, but we feel Ceddy being sent away has been tough on both of you."

His son scraped at the ground with his bare foot, "I dunno what's wrong, but I just feel sorta yuck lately. It's like the day after your birthday, you know things are jake but it's not like it was before."

"Your mother, for once, is all for moving and while I don't mind it here, there is something about this town that just doesn't sit right with me."

Again John kicked at the ground, this time picking a stone up with his toes and flicking it away. "I reckon we wouldn't be squibs if we went to another town, 'cause everybody here knows that we aren't yella bellies."

His father smiled and told him, "I am sure that nobody thinks that, but what people think is not important: it's what you think of yourself; that is what counts."

"Would we be living in town an' goin' to the town school?"

"Yes, the school is a bit bigger than this one but not as big as Ballon.

The town is on a gully but it wouldn't be like the river here because it is a long way from the sea and pretty dry."

John knew in his heart of hearts that their time here had run out. He also knew that establishing themselves in a new town and school would not be easy without the steadying influence and leadership of brother Charles, not that he was worried about the responsibility of looking after little brother Edward. No, what worried him was that by leaving he knew that his final link to his mate would be gone.

He looked up at his father, "Ya know, Dad, I reckon it's time we made a move. Maybe when Kondie gets out of jail you can get him a job at this other town and they kin come and live there."

"I think you are right son, it is time to move and I would give Kondie a job anywhere and anytime."

There was no more discussion regarding whether or not they were going to move and the family automatically went into 'packing up mode'. There were regrets, as this was as close to normal living the family had experienced and, while they were off side with a lot of the town, strong bonds had been established with those that agreed with their various stands and knew that the system needed changing.

On the day of leaving a small group came to say good bye, there were even a few tears, but after hugs and handshakes the little Austin headed south to a place that more than anywhere else John came to look upon as his home town.

CHAPTER FIVE

Turkey nest dam
THE OLD BRASS WHEEL

The Gully as it was affectionately known was a town of about six hundred but with one of the largest shires in the country. It had a state and convent school with the latter having boarding facilities for children from the outer cattle and sheep stations. Arthur was taking over as the shire overseer: the same position he had held in their last town but this place was different and, for once, the job just fitted the man and the man to the job. John's fears of settling in to a new town and school without his older brother were unfounded. Of course there were a few hiccups but these soon sorted themselves out.

The school's rugby league team welcomed both the boys as they had arrived in town just in time for the annual six match series against the Convent School. The State School had not won this contest for many years and with the arrival of the two newcomers the State kids saw a real chance to topple the mighty Convent boys. John was not new to the game and, while not particularly fast, his size, strength and natural ability made him perfect for the sport. Edward, even though he was four years younger and a lot smaller, also found a regular playing spot in the team.

There were unwritten rules within the teams that the bigger boys had to take it easy on the smaller members of the opposing side but this was based on size not age which was good for Edward who, unlike his brothers, was not big for his age. However, even in the first game of the series the Convent boys soon realised that the little full back, having grown up with two brothers quite a bit older then himself, could take it and dish it out with the best of them. He was particularly a fearless defender and the opposition quickly knew that the 'footy jumper with legs' would attach himself to any part of their person and just hang on until help arrived.

During one game a couple of weeks after they arrived an opposing forward who had trampled over Edward on his way to the try line and was a bit worried about the possibility of a payback said to John at half time, "Sorry I ran over your brother; he shoulda got out of the way like the other little kids."

"Nah, she's right, mate", came the reply, "He's pretty tough an' he nearly got ya. I only stick up for him when some big bloke thumps him an' I know it's unfair. You were goin' for a try, so no worries." This was the first time John had actually spoken to one of the Convent kids and he was curious about them. "My name's John, what's yours?"

"Me name's Alan but everyone calls me Skimmy; that's me nickname."

Before John could ask about the origin of the nickname, the whistle blew for the boys to return to the field for the battle to recommence. Later, when the game was over, John asked a couple of his team mates, "What's that Skimmy bloke like?"

Ginger, a kid he had pulled up with in their first week, replied "Ol' Skimmy, he's alright for a cattle tick. He lives just down the road from you. His old man works at the power house. Poor bloke's Mum's a real battle axe. She won't let him play with us State School kids; dunno why, but ya can go there an' swap comics if ya wanna."

"That's good t' know, 'cause I got a stack of comics that I've read a million times, so I might take a ganda at where he lives an' go there one arvo.

Life in 'The Gully' suited the whole family and, because the town was a large rail head and centre for an area the size of Victoria, it had more than the usual number of transients as part of the population. This meant that by virtue of their numbers, the non-locals, especially at the State School, did not experience the parochialism of other small western towns. True, the boys had to work a little harder when it came to entertaining themselves but life in numerous road camps had prepared them well for this.

It was on one particularly hot and boring Saturday afternoon that John and his mate Ginger sat on the verandah watching old Tommo's mail truck disappear into the shimmering heat. Looking out towards the north the only visible signs of life other than the mail truck slowly groaning its way out of town via the road past the cemetery, were the hawks circling over the rubbish tip. The tip was a great place to go and, while it was supposed to be out of bounds, the boys and their friends were there on a regular basis. Their main purpose was to scrounge. Non-returnable bottles could be lined up and smashed with stones and the returnable ones were collected and taken to the local soft drink factory whose owner paid four shillings a hundred for them.

On this particular day the town's inhabitants, save a few, sheltered inside away from the blistering Queensland summer sun. One of those to brave the 110° in the 'bloody shade' thermal blast, was Mad Mick. The boys sitting on the verandah watched Mick as he steadily weaved his way home after being tossed out of both the top and bottom pubs. His exclusion from the town's two watering holes was due solely to his lack of funds, not his already inebriated condition. Mad Mick was the town's resident drunk. Mind you, not that there weren't plenty of others with the same love of the amber fluid but Mick's notorious Race Day and St Patrick's Day binges that almost always ended in hospital with the D.T.s, had not only reduced the once proud name of Michael Kevin Patrick O'Connell to a simple Mad Mick but also made sure that he maintained the title of 'The Gully's number one boozer'.

When sober enough, Mick rode a bike and the boys knew there was a shilling to be made by back-tracking his movements, finding where the ancient machine had been thrown down in drunken disgust, and returning it to its owner.

"Hey Mr. O'Connell can we get ya bike for ya?" called one of the boys.

"To be sure lad" replied Mick, his Irish brogue even thicker with the drink. "But you'll be getting yer shillin' another day if that's OK wid ya."

The boys knew that Mick would certainly be good for the bob and waved their agreement rather than engage the Irishman in further conversation, knowing that, from past experience, this could include Mick's life story or his version of the troubles in Ireland, neither of which had interested the boys even the first time they had heard them.

"We'd better go now before Skimmy Campbell or one of his Convent mates gets Mick's bike first." said Ginger pulling his old felt hat even further over his shock of red hair.

"Skimmy's not allowed to go to Mad Mick's hut" replied John or Blondie, as most of the town called him.

Ginger looked up from trying to remove a Christ-thorn from the sole of his foot "Ya wouldn't wanna bet on that would ya. I seen him and Jacko there plenty a times."

"Jacko I agree, but ol' Skimmy, I don't think so. His mum'd smack him until his nose bled if she caught him." came John's reply, nodding knowingly.

The third member of the trio suddenly reached down picked up a stone and threw it with amazing accuracy at a cat making a short cut through the yard. With a loud squawk the poor animal leapt back over the fence to the relative safety of his own territory on the other side.

"Jesus! Barry!" exclaimed John "If my Mum hadda seen ya clobber the Browns' cat ya might have been barred, an' that would have been nothing to what Mrs Brown would have done if she seen it come flying back into her yard screaming like that."

"Yeah." nodded Ginger, "But it was a bloody good shot though don't cha reckon."

"Didn't say it wasn't a top shot; it's just that when you blokes clobber their cat the Dragon tells Mum and I am the one who cops it."

"Sorry mate, but at home me old man reckons that if that cat pisses in our garage again he will make a tennis racquet out of it."

"A tennis racquet?" the other two inquired together, their minds imagining Barry's father squashing the Browns' cat to the extent that he could somehow mould it into the desired shape.

"I'm not sure what he meant but that's what he said."

As if a joint decision had been made, the three ambled through the back yard and set off in the general direction that Mad Mick had come from. The trip to the bottom pub took about twenty minutes owing to a slight delay while they exchanged pleasantries with a group of boys who lived at Sacred Heart Convent Boarding School. It is true that the trio had not followed the most direct route and it is true that they did know that there would probably be some Convent boarders playing under the shady trees in the front of the school. They also knew that no matter how big or how many there were, they could give as much lip to them as they wanted, as none would dare leave the confines of the Convent yard.

Barry called out, "Convent! Convent! Ring the bell then turn around and march to hell."

The reply came straight back, "State State sittin' on a log eating bellies out of frogs."

The banter back and forward was, for the better part, pretty harmless and was more a point scoring exercise. What they did not take into account was Father Garvey quietly coming up from behind and putting the fear of the Almighty into the State School boys. Although none of the trio was of the Catholic faith, you did not have to be, to know, and more importantly, to respect the good Father.

"Sorry Sir," they stammered and quickly headed off towards the original destination of the Bottom Pub.

"Gee, fancy being so deaf that we didn't hear ol' Garvey comin'." said John.

"I reckon he just sorta drifted over like a ghost. Priests can do that sort of thing ya know, that's why we never heard a thing."

"Awe pull me other leg Barry, although he has sorta got an evil eye." Ginger retorted.

The pubs were, as usual on a Saturday afternoon, doing a roaring trade. A couple of the bigger shearing sheds had cut out as well, so this swelled the number of hard seasoned drinkers. The boys skirted around the overflow on the footpath and went straight to the galvanized iron toilet block at the rear of the main building, expecting, as usual, to find Mick's bike there.

Now, it was there alright, but not in the state that the boys had expected it to be found. The old Malvin Star normally showed as much wear and tear as its owner, but this time another one of the hotel's patrons had driven right over the centre of the frame and the whole thing was now jammed up under the rear axle of the offending Utility. The driver of the Ute was sitting at the wheel muttering to himself something about rubbish which shouldn't be left around where a man could drive over it. The boys knew the driver's reputation and did not want to get on the wrong side of Blackie Burns, so their approach to him was with extreme caution, making sure that there was a clear getaway path. "G'day Mr. Burns, looks like ya run over ole Mick's bike. We were just coming to get it for him."

Burns looked hard at John "You're Blondie aren't ya - Arthur's boy?"

"Yes." stammered John worried that Blackie had concentrated on him and, to make things worse, knew who he was.

"I reckon he wouldn't be too bloody happy if he knew you was hanging around the pub, knowing Arthur as I do." The look on John's face confirmed that Blackie was right. "I'll tell ya what, if Mick doesn't find out who ran over his bloody old heap of garbage your old man won't find out you was hanging around here."

At that, he flicked his cigarette butt out the window and with the grinding of metal he drove off the bike and out the gate.

The boys looked at the mangled remains. "Pump still looks okay" said Ginger picking it out of the twisted frame. "Only bloody thing that is, that's for sure." Barry grunted trying to turn the buckled front wheel with his big toe.

"I reckon old Mick is gonna spew when we show him this mess, an' I reckon somehow or other we'll get into strife." said John still worried over the fact that Blackie Burns had recognised him.

"Let's just leave this heap of rubbish an' pretend that we decided not to come." muttered Barry nodding in agreement with what John had said.

"Yep. Let's just go for a swim down the Turkey Nest an' let Mad Mick find out from someone else." Ginger concluded.

The boys figured an illegal swim in the tepid bore water of the town Turkey Nest dam was a good substitute for the hassles that would be involved in getting Mick's damaged bike out to his shack on the edge of town. The Turkey Nest was called so because it was a dam built above the ground in the shape of a bush turkey nest. Always fed from an artesian bore, these dams allowed the water time to cool prior to going into the stock watering troughs. However, the walls of these are not made to have people clambering around them, hence, the no-go zone for the boys. Luckily the dam was out on its own about half a mile from town so, as long as they kept a look out, they were not in a lot of danger of being caught by the local Ranger or the Sergeant doing his rounds.

First choice for a swim was always the local creek but the drought had reduced it to a series of muddy puddles that had about six inches of water and eighteen inches of mud. Mind you, if desperate, the boys would go there to cool off.

The boys found the water in the Turkey Nest was warm as usual but they didn't mind this, as there was a breeze and by repeatedly getting in and out they were cooled using the same evaporation principal of the old butter safe. Soon after they arrived their attention was drawn to a battered old truck slowly making its way towards the dam. They knew the truck was not local and for that reason alone were not unduly worried but to be on the safe side they pulled their shirts and shorts close to the edge where they were lying just in case a quick retreat was called for. With the screech of metal on metal giving testament to the non-existence of any brake linings the old Ford shuddered to a halt.

As the dust settled, two blue cattle dogs jumped off the back and started to sniff their way around the existing campsite. A few moments later one of the occupants slid from behind the steering wheel nearly landing on one of the dogs, it in turn raced excitedly around as if trying to get a good sniff of everything before the area was contaminated by the smells bought by himself and his travelling companions. The passenger took a crutch from the shelf under the rear window of the truck and, in a much practiced action clamped it into his left armpit and climbed out as nimbly as he would have done fifteen years before when he had two legs. He whistled to the dog that was making its way towards where the boys were hidden at the top of the Turkey Nest "Gorn! Git under the damn truck ya bloody mongrel." he said trying to give it a clout with his crutch as it zipped by him to the comparative safety under the trailer that was being towed behind the truck.

The boys watched the goings-on below them. "Reckon they are drovers." whispered Ginger. Barry shook his head "Not a lot of gear an only two dogs".

John joined in the conversation "Could be poddy dodgers. The old man said there's been a lot goin' on lately."

"You galah they ain't poddy dodgers. Ya gotta have somewhere to put 'em if you're poddy dodging." Barry said, not without authority, as his father was known to add the odd stray calf to his own herd from time to time.

By this time, the two men had pulled enough gear from the truck to establish in the boys' minds that the newcomers intended to stay, at least, for a while. The fire was started and Hoppy, as his mate called him, went to the pipe for the cattle trough and filled a blackened old billy with water. On his way back, he glanced up at the Turkey Nest and called out, "Hope you bloody kids haven't been pissin' in the water."

The boys looked at each other in panic, "Jesus! He has seen us." said Ginger and Barry together with the redhead continuing, "If we took off for the creek they wouldn't catch us that's for sure."

The boys knew full well that if they made a run for it those below would never get near them but they also knew that the men could probably give a description of the boys. In a town the size of 'The Gully' even blind Freddie would know who they were describing. Summing up the situation John said, "Let's just go down and talk. I reckon we'll be able to tell if they are going to dob us in or not."

At this the boys gathered up their clothes, dressed and ambled down the side of the Turkey Nest to where the men were still setting up their camp. "'G'day" they said as one. The one legged man looked up from his task of laying out his swag roll. "Wot you kids doin' swimming in the Nest? Don't ya know the stock inspector or the local sarge would kick ya up the bum if he caught ya?"

The boys scuffed the dirt with their bare feet until John spoke "Yes we know, but the stock inspector, old Herb, is out with a mob of cattle and the Sarge never comes out here; he's kept too busy at the pubs at this time of the day."

By now the second man had finished setting up a trestle table and joined the conversation, "Ya say the local sarge don't come out here much?"

The boys, happy to have the subject changed nodded, Barry adding "I ain't never seen him here. He's fat an' he don't do much because he gets the chaff: so me mum reckons anyway."

During the conversation the two men continued to organise themselves. The boys, all veterans of numerous camps, were most impressed with their speed and the efficient way the task was being accomplished.

"Wotcha doin' here?" Ginger asked the one legged man.

He exchanged glances with his mate, took a packet of ready rubbed tobacco from the pocket of his battered Queensland Railway issue shirt and told the boys, "Me an' Bluey are dealers in non-ferrous metals."

The terminology was obviously confusing so after a moment's hesitation John ventured, "Barry's old man is a cattle dealer, is that sorta like what you are?"

By this time Hoppy had finished rolling himself a cigarette and after surveying his handiwork he stuck it in the corner of his mouth pulled a stick out of the fire and lit up and a couple of obviously satisfying drags later he said, "Ya on the right track young fella but lift up the tarp on the trailer an' see what we deal in."

The boys cautiously lifted the canvas sheet dropping it almost immediately upon viewing the contents, "It's just a load of old rubbish." said Barry "Wotcha want to cart that around for?"

By this time the billy had boiled and the other man Bluey added the tea leaves. He then thumped the side of the can to help them to settle to the bottom. Taking a minute from the task at hand he told the boys "If you know what you're looking for you can make a few quid picking up old rubbish."

An astute reader of faces he saw the boys' interest change at the mention of being able to pick up a few quid. He let that sink in as he poured the strong black tea into two chipped enamel panicans then held the can up in an offer to the boys, who refused with a shake of their heads. Hoppy put a heaped teaspoon of powdered milk and two of sugar into his mug and cranked vigorously. Bluey, on the other hand, took his as it came: hot and black. "Yep I reckon that little lot is worth about a thousand quid." he said nonchalantly. "We pick it up out here and cart it to the coast and sell it."

"Git out! ya pulling me leg!" Barry said, having another look under the tarp on the trailer. "There's lotsa rubbish around here an' I'll bet ya won't go around and pick it all up."

Bluey slurped his scalding hot tea. "Look boys, there is good and bad rubbish; the good stuff is worth a bit, though not a lot mind you. The trouble is me and ol' Hoppy have seen a few too many Xmas dinners an' now life ain't so easy."

His eyes went from the boys to his one legged friend, who on cue, struggled to rise and put the pot of potatoes he had peeled on the fire. "Yep, it has not been easy for the old bloke since he lost a leg fighting the Japs an' I done me back in carrying him from fifty miles behind enemy lines and down the Kokada trail to hospital."

The boys were impressed. They had heard of the Kokada Trail at the numerous Anzac Day parades they had been required to attend. John had actually been to the bottom end of the trail and visited the stark war cemetery nearby; this, together with numerous war films they all had seen, gave the boys a fair idea of what it was like. Bluey sensed this and went on, "Yep, we fought the Japs for years so that young blokes like you lot could be free. Not much to show for it though: a one legged cripple an' me with a busted back." He pushed his battered hat to the back of his head and looking to the heavens gave a deep sigh. Hoppy spoke with a slow gravelly voice. "For sure, nobody wants to help two old diggers who spent ten years up to their arm pits in the jungle mud fighting the bloody nips. But between us we manage to scrape together enough to put tucker on the table."

John while impressed was interested in one point "How come you was fighting the Japs for ten years? I didn't think the war went on for that long."

The men glanced at each other before Bluey answered. "Special forces we were, started fighting the Japs years before the government said we was at war."

Hoppy made a point of pulling up his trouser leg and giving his stump a good rub, "Yep, this is all I have got to show, but at least you kids are free and won't have to work in the slave farms the Japs had planned to set in Australia."

"Slave farms! Wot slave farms?" The boys stammered.

Here Bluey cut in, "Hoppy, ya not allowed to talk about them slave farms for kids: we signed the special secrets law remember."

"Damn well forgot. Sorry mate. I reckon the pain the old stump give me after a days' hard yakka causes problems with me old brain."

At this point Hoppy turned to Barry "Be a mate and get me bloody tin leg out of the truck it's under the seat. Oh! and get the bottle of goanna oil that's in the glove box."

This did it, the boys were now completely in awe of these 'battle-hardened old diggers' and ready to do their bit to help the cause. Mind you, the prospect of earning a few shilling was also a factor that had been quickly entered into the equation.

"Ya reckon there might be some of that good rubbish around The Gully?" asked John, quickly adding "You know the sort that might be worth a few shillin's, if a bloke was to bring it to ya?"

Bluey patted his top pocket, at the same time looking over at his mate, "Toss us the makings will ya cobber." The butt of his last cigarette was split open and the remaining tobacco was mixed with the fresh that he took from the packet that Hoppy had thrown to him. He made two, one going behind his ear and the other into his mouth. Then, using his bare fingers he plucked a red hot ember from the fire and lit up. Once sure it was properly alight he flipped the coal back into the fire.

The three boys had all seen this done before, especially by drovers whose fingers are as tough as the leather they handled day in and day out. However, that didn't mean they did not make a note of it even though they knew it had been done to impress them. Hoppy took the tin leg and bottle of oil putting a little on the joint at the knee before taking a cupped handful and rubbing it into the stump of his leg. "Ya know Blue these boys look like they are smart enough for us to consider taking them into the business; sorta like as junior partners." He continued to rub his stump while his mate appeared to be deep in thought over the proposal, "Gee Hop I know it's gettin' hard for you to get around. But the cost of our time to train these boys and the amount of scrap around, I just don't know if it would be worth our while."

The hook was baited and the boys went for it hook, line and sinker, they assured the men that there was an abundance of scrap in The Gully and they would learn quickly what was good and what was not.

Bluey then clinched the deal. "Look boys, its true me old mate here has a bit of trouble from the stump and me with the jungle fever coming back more and more, we don't pick up what we did a few years ago. So a bit of local labour will help. Oh! We'll pay ya a decent quid, don't worry, especially for the top quality stuff."

The training as it was called took all of twenty minutes, the boys were then given a very rough idea of what they could earn for various metals and that it all had to be brought to the camp. They were also told the best places to look and what were ready sources like old batteries for lead, radiators for copper, old taps for brass and pots and pans for aluminum.

Every afternoon after school for the next week the boys spent scrounging through the town tip. It did not, however, take them long to realise that "good scrap" was not as easy to find as they had been told. Most of the stuff they carted out to the camp was rejected as not worth paying for, the only sure money was old batteries and the boys earned three pence each for these.

They could only fit four on their billy cart which the one and a half mile trip from the tip to the men's camp earned them a shilling. Also, most times the boys went there the men were in town on business so if the boys were sure to be paid they had to wait for the men to return. These delays and the lack of payment for the rejected scrap (which went on the truck anyway) soon made the young entrepreneurs start to question the economics of the whole business. On the Friday they were all at John's house discussing the future. "I reckon they are sticking it to us." said John between mouthfuls of a vegemite sandwich. Ginger nodded his agreement "Bloody oath, ya see that stuff that they reckon is no good? Well they don't chuck it, oh no, it still goes on the truck along with the rest."

Barry agreed with his mates but still held out hope that they would get lucky, "Ya know," he said "Those blokes are interested in two things: one is solid brass stuff and the other is where the old Sarge is and what he does."

"Yeah." agreed John. "Old Hoppy was pretty happy when I told him the Sarge played golf on a Sunday arvo." Changing the subject he continued, "Forget that; let's go to the old foundry an' see if there is anything worth picking up there."

The foundry had been closed for years and belonged to a station owner named Newton. He had once caught the boys playing there and had dobbed to their parents. As a result the place was officially out of bounds. Not that this worried the boys a great deal, as they played and explored there regularly. This trip however had a purpose and to their surprise yielded a treasure beyond their wildest dreams. There leaning against the rear wall was an old pulley wheel nine inches wide, four feet in diameter and made of solid brass. It was so heavy that the only way the boys could move the thing was by rolling it.

They made no attempt to disguise their actions as they did not look on what they were doing as stealing. On the contrary they felt sure that Mr. Newton would be happy to see the end of some of the rubbish lying around.

The wheel was too big and too heavy for their cart so it was decided that, the next day being Saturday, they would roll it out to the camp. This proved to be no mean feat and one that took nearly all morning. Time and time again it fell on its side and had to be righted, one boy stood on each side to keep it up and the other pushed it along from behind. Each time it toppled over whoever was on that side literally had to jump for his life. Initially they had tried to roll it with a piece of old pipe through it like an axle. However the first time they lost control using this method, Ginger finished with his arm trapped underneath and John tore his hand open when he was catapulted across the wheel. They freed Ginger's arm, which didn't suffer a lot because it had depressed into the soft soil. John's hand was wrapped in his shirt and bled continually as they struggled to get the wheel to its destination. As they got nearer their expectations of wealth grew with each weary step. Finally, they reached the truck and with a huge sigh let the huge wheel thump to the ground for the last time.

The two war heroes who had watched the boys struggling for the last half-mile or so came around to inspect their trophy. After a scratch at it with an old file Bluey grunted and said, "Not a very good quality brass in that ol' wheel, only worth a couple of quid but seein' ya worked so hard to get it here I'll give ya a quid each."

The boys were gutted and John, who would normally never question an adult exploded, "A bloody quid each! That must weigh at least eighty pounds and at the price ya told us its gotta be a least four quid each."

At this point Hoppy spoke "If ya reckon we are doin' ya over well just take the bloody wheel and piss off out of here." He waited for what he had said to sink in, "Gorn piss off! We don't want the bloody wheel."

The boys knew they had no choice and reluctantly nodded their agreement to the deal, the money was paid and the trio set off for John's place to get his still bleeding hand looked at. They tramped through the house to the kitchen at the rear; neither parent was home so after a bit of a clean, the wound was properly inspected for the first time.

"Reckon it'll need a couple a stitches mate," said Barry.

Ginger nodded in agreement "Ol' Matron will probably give ya a shot as well, 'cause the end of that pipe was pretty grubby an' that's where tetanus comes from."

John agreed that the old "Battle Axe" had better have a look at his hand but hoping he would need neither stitching nor a tetanus shot, it was not to be. After a good clean out, five stitches were needed, as was a shot in the rump. After the repair work was finished the Matron said "I've spoken to your Mother young man and she wants to see you straight home."

John was only too happy to be out of the Matron's clutches. "Yes Matron, I'm gonna go straight home now." adding as he reached the door "'An thanks for fixin' me up."

On the way home John had time to reflect on a day that had started out to hold high hopes yet had turned out to be a total disaster. He was not to know that on a scale of one to ten, the day, to that moment had been a ten.

It was getting late when he dumped his bike on the verandah and hoped to just blend in with his brothers and parents as they were all in the kitchen while dinner was being prepared. As he entered, the look on his parents' faces told him that blending was out of the question and survival was probably more important. As his young brother took off, not wanting to be caught in the cross fire, John knew he was in trouble, but wasn't sure what for. He had left a mess when he cleaned himself up before going to the hospital, but knew it was worse than that. His shirt was probably ruined but it wasn't one of his better ones and under the circumstances he felt that, at most, he would get a talking to for that. No, experience told him that when his parents joined forces on one of his misdemeanors he was in big strife

His father broke the silence "Mr. Newton has just left."

John's heart fell through the floor and the blood drained from his face.

"Yep, he said you, Barry and Ginger stole a valuable brass wheel from his old foundry." He took his time to roll a cigarette and John knew better than to say a word. "Well?" he grunted, lighting up.

By now Johns brain was in full survival mode. "It was leaning against the wall an' was just ol' scrap that no one wanted."

"You know the foundry is out of bounds, and as for just being old scrap Mr. Newton said it was worth at least twenty pounds."

"It wasn't worth that much 'cause it was poor quality an' we only got three quid." John said holding his damaged hand in hope to divert some of the attention away from the subject.

Getting the hint, his mother spoke for the first time. "Matron tells me your hand will be fine." At this he knew from the tone and the finality of the statement that, while down the track his hand might attract some sympathy, it would not feature in the present conversation. It was obvious that the battle was lost and the only thing left was to get as much as possible out of the terms of surrender. Knowing that he was not coming from a position of strength John made a clean breast of the whole scrap metal business.

As the story of the boys' venture into the world of non-ferrous metal unfolded, his parents could not help being just a little proud, not that they let this show of course. He concluded by explaining how they had only received a pound each for the wheel and he was sure as it was not good quality brass the dealers would probably be happy to sell it back to them. His parents agreed that this course of action was a very sensible one as then the wheel could be returned to Mr. Newton. However, his Father also added, "If the wheel is not returned then you and your mates will have to pay the twenty pounds that the wheel is valued at."

"And don't think the matter is finished if and when the wheel is returned." said his mother "No pocket money for two weeks and washing up and chopping the wood for a month. Also you will spend two Saturdays working for Mr. Newton at his cattle yards, without pay of course."

John would have much preferred a belting as punishment, painful for a while but then over and done with. This way the pain would linger with him long after the events of today were forgotten by everyone else. That night sleep did not come easily as the thought of having to transport the wheel back to Mr. Newton's shed was not a task that he was looking forward to. By about ten the next morning the three were on their way back to the Turkey Nest. Bluey and Hoppy were not particularly happy to see them but listened while the boys explained their plight. "Of course, you can buy it back." said Bluey. "Always willin' to help out."

Much relieved the boys handed back the three one pound notes they had been given the day before. Hoppy looked at the crumpled notes in Gingers hand saying, "Ya don't think we are goin' t' sell for the same price as we bought it for do yaw?"

Blue continued "Gee that wouldn't be good business. Gee! Got to live yaw know. So you bugger off and find about another seventeen quid an' she's yours again."

John tried desperately to point out that the wheel was not theirs to sell and how much trouble the three of them were in as a result of their actions. The men were not interested in their pleas and to make matters worse, Bluey told the boys, "An' ya better get organised 'cause tomorra we'll be gone."

Hoppy closed the matter as a Ute pulled up with a couple of ringers that the boys knew by sight. "Yep that's the deal. Now clear out as we got a bit a business t' do an ya ain't welcome here."

Still dazed, the boys wandered off to the other side of the Turkey Nest to discuss their bleak future amongst themselves. "Might as well be a thousand as seventeen quid." said Barry. "A gun shearer only gets forty on a good week. So what chance have we got of getting seventeen?"

Ginger was picking at the cracked skin on his heels with an old pocketknife. "I got one pound and six shillings in me school bank plus this quid here." he said.

John nodded as if agreeing that their savings would have to be used to pay their debt. "I got about a fiver counting this quid here. Wot you got Baz?"

"Gee ya both know I just used all me savings as my part of the new bike I got for me birthday. An' now I am bloody skint; only got about ten John plus this quid here."

They did not need to be geniuses in maths to know that their total was still short by over half of the required amount. In desperation Barry suggested "I reckon we could sneak out here tonight an' pinch the wheel back. We can leave the three quid so they couldn't tell the Sarge."

The other two pondered on this for a while before agreeing that this might be the only course of action left open to them. They knew the habits of the two men pretty well by now and could bank on them being at the pub between six and ten o'clock. After some discussion John put their final plan into words. "If they leave the camp at six we'll grab the wheel straight away. We will never be able to get it far before we will all have to go home for dinner so I reckon we'll just have to hide it."

"Great idea." said Ginger "Then we can come here tomorra an' pick it after they go."

Barry agreed, "Yep they might not even look to check their load 'cause it's already tied down under a tarp. But we'll probably have to dump it in the Turkeys Nest otherwise they might see it just by accident."

The thought of fishing the huge wheel out of the foot deep mud in the bottom of the dam did give John some problems but not wanting to dampen his friends enthusiasm, he said nothing. In truth just getting the wheel up the side of the Turkeys Nest was going to be a feat in its self. During their discussion on how they were going to recover the wheel the boys had not noticed that another four vehicles had arrived at the camp. On seeing this they went to the top of the Nest for a better view of the proceedings, "Now I know why they were so interested in what the Sarge was doing." said Ginger They're runnin' a two-up game."

"Too right." agreed Barry "Gees! Wouldn't ya know it? Ol' man Newtons there! He should ask them blokes for his bloody wheel. Save us the trouble of pinching it back for him."

They soon tired with watching the game and set off towards the creek in search of something to fill their time until the game finished and, hopefully, Bluey and Hoppy had enough money to buy up big at the pub. As they wandered away they noticed another vehicle approaching the Turkey Nest only this one was coming across country and was hidden from the two-up players by the dam.

"Bloody hell it's the Sarge!" said John "He's gonna catch 'em!"

As the police vehicle pulled into the camp from around the blind side of the dam all hell broke loose with people and cars going in all directions. By this time the boys had returned to the top of the Turkey Nest and watched the proceedings with a great deal of interest. As the local upholder of the law, Sergeant Murphey, took his job seriously, especially when it involved outsiders. As was usual in these cases of illegal gaming, the proceedings of the game were confiscated and the perpetrators were given their marching orders: effective immediately.

It was surprising just how quickly the men broke camp and what little effect their pleas to, "Give us a break." had. It suddenly dawned on the boys that not only would the men depart but so would the precious cargo that they had hoped to return to its rightful owner. Quietly the prospect of involving the law in their problem was discussed but decided against: not that a proper hearing wouldn't be given, it was just that this was their problem and would be dealt with by them.

Bluey and Hoppy literally threw the last of their belongings into the truck, nodded curtly to the man in uniform and climbed into the cab. The started motor ground away until it seemed that the battery was spent, the boys watched in hope that the ancient engine would refuse to cooperate with the order to leave. But the men knew that if they were not to leave in their vehicle then alternative transport would soon be supplied. This, however, would only take them as far as the police station. Anyway, they were accustomed to the problems involved with getting "The bloody heap of rubbish" up and running. Bluey alighted, undid the eight gauge wire that secured the bonnet. He then laid it back against the windscreen and removed the air cleaner from the top of the carburetor.

Using his hand to completely choke the engine, he yelled to Hoppy, "OK mate kick 'er in the guts now." Almost immediately it fired, coughed a couple of times then roared into life. The air cleaner was thumped back into position with the palm of his hand and the bonnet let fall with a crash. The eight gauge wire was reinstalled and, minutes later, the boys watched the truck turn away from the town upon reaching the main road. The police vehicle that had followed to that point went the other way and disappeared almost immediately behind the first row of houses.

From their slightly elevated position on the Turkey Nest the boys were able to watch the truck for some time, perhaps hoping that it would stop near enough to town for them to recover their loss but this was not to be and as it disappeared into the shimmering mirage on the horizon, the boys at last accepted their fate. Barry knew now that his parents would soon become involved. He also knew that his punishment would be similar to what John had received.

However, they all knew that Ginger's parents' punishment for his part in their business could, at the very least, be a flogging. John could read this in his mate's face and immediately his mind went back to the last time his friend had been punished, and his own involvement in the incident.

Ginger had broken a window at school and the headmaster had gone to his father during the lunch period and asked for him to pay for it to be repaired. The teacher knew the man's reputation for drunken violence and had he have not been such a pompous fool he would have been more sensitive to the outcome of his actions. That afternoon the boys were working on their bikes at Ginger's house when his father came home from the pub. He was drunk and in a nasty mood. Without saying a word he walked up to his son and punched him in the face. The boy fell immediately to the ground rolling into a ball to protect himself from the kicks that he knew were to come.

John tried to reason with the man as he screamed abuse about "broken windows costing money" while trying to get a decent kick at his son curled up on the dirt floor of the shed. Never in his life had John witnessed an attack like this and as a last resort he stood between the drunk and his son. He had no idea what he was going to do only that he wanted somehow to help his mate. For a brief moment man and boy locked eyes. "So Blondie wants his arse kicked too does he? Well I am just the guy to do it."

John looked down to see if his friend had managed to move out of range and at that moment a sledgehammer blow caught him in the ribs under his heart. He has only a vague recollection of the events that followed but was aware of a lot of screaming and shouting as more people involved themselves in the fracas.

The end result was that Ginger had a dislocated shoulder and a broken nose while John had a friend for life and a very sore ribcage. His parents wanted the man charged with assault but decided against it after talking to the police and giving consideration to the effect police involvement could have on Ginger.

The Sergeant did have a word, not that this was deterrent enough to stop the man thumping his wife and kids when the mood took him, but at least he knew that there were people around that cared and if necessary would take action.

Thoughts of that terrifying afternoon flooded back as John saw the panic in his friend's eyes. "Don't worry mate; me and Barry 'ill be the only ones in the can. Ya old man will never know."

The tears that had started to form were quickly sniffed away, and in an act of bravado, Ginger said, "She's right he don't scare me no more, an' I can look after meself."

"Yep we know ya can mate, but why should three of us get inta trouble?. It is only smart for one of us to miss out if possible, don't ya reckon?" said John in an of-handed sort of a way.

"Maybe, but next time one o' you can miss getting into strife." came the stammered but thankful reply.

"Natch." said Barry "It's my turn ta miss out next time."

At this point the boys decided to venture to the now deserted campsite to take a look and see if anything had been left behind. Again, his usual cheery self Ginger told his friends "I went to a two-up site once an' found a few bob what had been dropped an' 'cause these guys left in a real rush we might get lucky."

"We could certainly do with a bit of good luck 'cause we certainly had our share of the other kind lately." said Barry as he looked at the foot prints to work out where the ring of men had stood.

Once the actual ring area of the game had been established the boys crouched down and started to scour the loose soil. Almost immediately Ginger found a ten shilling note and minutes later found another. All three of them picked up a few coins of various denominations until John found a penny. Not thinking too much about it he carried on looking until Ginger announced that he had found a penny also. At this time John took the original penny and put it beside the one his friend had just found.

"Jesus!" he muttered "Both are 1901 Boadicea pennies! These are 'specially used for two-up. This is why those blokes tried to talk the Sarge into letting them have a bit of time to clean up."

"Ya know" said Barry, "I've heard me old man talking about a good set of these pennies being worth a few quid."

The boys did not have to be told that they would have to find the third penny, so they immediately set about searching the entire area. An hour or so later they decided that it was pointless to continue any longer but in the process of looking for the penny, they had found quite a bit of loose change and they sat down to count up their loot. John's battered hat had been placed in the centre and everything, save the two pennies, were dumped into it. At any other time finding almost three pounds would have been reason for great celebration and, while it did lift the dark cloud a little, their spirits were still at an all-time low. This was unusual for the trio as they normally lived each day to the hilt and be dammed about tomorrow.

Obviously the long term commitment of having to pay for the brass wheel weighed heavily on their minds; including what they had just found they were still short by about ten pounds. To add to their woes Barry announced, "We won't be able to get the money in your bank Ginger, 'cause ya old man has to sign the slip an' he'll want to know wotcha gonna do with it."

"Bloody hell! I forgot about that. Well I reckon I'm dead meat."

"Forget the money in ya bank, we weren't goin' ta tell ya old man before we found this money here. So we are actually ahead of where we were an' that is not counting the money in ya bank." said John taking the money from his hat before returning it to his head. Ginger objected to the idea of not being to be able to contribute but in his heart knew that his friend's actions would save him a lot of grief. John's attention, however, was drawn to the circle that the crown of his hat had made in the loose soil. "Well I'll be a monkey's uncle!" he exclaimed. There, right in the centre of the ring made by his hat, was the third penny. It had obviously been made visible by the action of putting down and picking up the hat.

A quick examination of the coin confirmed what they had hoped for, it was another 1901 Boadicea.

The boys set off for Barry's place as they figured that his father, Clarrie, would be the right man to talk to with regard to selling their find. Clarrie Hardy was a huge man - probably six foot four inches and seventeen stone in weight - but the thing that people remember about him was the size and strength of his hands. Local legend has it that during a fight a shearer had tried to king hit him. Clarrie stopped the blow by grabbing the man's arm half way between elbow and wrist. Normally a gentle giant, he was happy to just hold the man at arm's length so he couldn't do any damage but angered by being held at bay like a child, the man used his teeth to try to free himself. The harder he bit the harder Clarrie squeezed, blood flowing freely with neither man willing to give in. The whole bar watched in morbid fascination until a quite audible crack preceded a scream of pain and terror. The shearer dropped to his knees clutching at his shattered arm, a later x-ray showed that both bones were fractured. Yet these same hands had gently delivered his son into this world when floods had made it impossible for the flying doctor to land at their remote cattle station.

He held the coins one at a time under the light turning them over checking for scratches as well as the serrations on their edges.

"Well I'll tell ya one thing they are a bloody side better than my set, of that I'm damn sure."

Ginger ventured, "Do ya reckon someone'll want t' buy 'em Mr. Hardy?"

"This set is as near perfect as I have seen for a while. What with the races being on in two weeks it will be the time to get a good price. 'N I know a couple of wild boys who will definitely be interested."

Seeing the boy's face drop at the mention of the two week delay he asked. "What is the hurry for the cash?" The ensuing silence made him push for further details. "Come on you blokes what the bloody hell ya been up to now?"

Barry decided that now was as good a time as any and told his father the whole story - of course omitting that they had planned to steal the wheel back. When he had concluded, Clarrie turned to the other two. "I figure your parents know about this, Blondie, and yours don't Ginger?"

Both nodded, "Well Barry 'll get the same strife as you Blondie 'cause I'll talk to Arthur. I know you'll want t' keep this from your old man Ginger but, to keep things fair, I'll arrange for ya to do some unpaid jobs for old Mrs Byrne. OK with you?"

Again the reply was quickly nodded, but he then asked. "How much do ya reckon we'll get if ya could sell them before the races?"

The big man contemplated Ginger's question while continuing to turn the pennies over in his hand, perhaps deciding to let the trio squirm a little before answering.

"I've seen a good set sell for ten quid an' I've heard of blokes paying ten quid each. It just depends on whether someone wants 'em bad enough."

All three did some quick arithmetic and knew that a tenner would see them clear of their debt, they would be broke but at this point were happy just to see the end of it all.

"Look boys, you leave the coins with me. I got a cobber who will definitely buy them. It will just be what he wants to pay that will be the question. So, you leave them with me an' I'll get the best price he is willing to pay on the spot."

The boys looked at each other and without speaking to each other agreed that this would be the best course of action.

"Don't worry boys she'll be right, with a bit of luck I'll see me mate tomorra an' ya could have ya dough in the arvo after school."

Monday always seemed to take a week to pass but this one was especially slow, not helped by an hour of religious instruction first thing in the morning. The town did not have a permanent non-Catholic member of the clergy, so when one did visit, the whole school, irrespective of denomination, was literally 'given the message.' Normally the boys didn't mind a break from the ordinary but today was different which meant that it just dragged and dragged. To make things worse the headmaster announced to the entire school, "It appears that we have a couple of clowns that borrowed Hazel's bike on Friday and I am telling you the offenders will be found and punished."

Hazel, the middle-aged school cleaner, had two loves; one was her job and the other was her bike. She was a fiery woman of Latin decent to whom nature had not been at all kind and as a result the poor woman was often on the receiving end of school yard pranks. Despite these physical handicaps her speed over ten yards was legendary and as a result many had felt the Government issued broom handle across their rear end. For reasons only known to her, Hazel would not enter the male toilets and this was her Achilles heel. Anyone fearful of getting a mop or broom wrapped around their head could always seek refuge there. The beloved bike was usually kept in sight but occasionally it would be taken for a joy ride and finish up in the male toilet. Then, from a safe vantage point, the perpetrator could watch the poor woman's embarrassment as she tried to retrieve her bike without looking and with as little as possible of her person entering the toilet.

That particular Friday was different. The bike had not ended up in its usual place but had been used to go to the shop. Thinking the bike was there but out of her reach Hazel had gone to the headmaster to retrieve it for her and the offender, seeing Hazel and the head master together, had dumped the bike at the school gate and fled. The headmaster considered, wrongly if the truth be known, that only the boys from grades six, seven and eight were capable of misusing the cleaner's bike and was determined to punish the offender.

"All the six, seven and eight boys out the front!" he barked. His dislike for boys of this age group was obvious in the way he spoke to them. "Now, I know one of you grubs pinched the bike and I really should go to the police. But, if the offender owns up, punishment will be administered by myself and the law will not be involved."

The threat of talking to the Sergeant had been used on numerous occasions and only indicated that the punishment would be the maximum he was allowed to administer. All those under threat knew that the offender would receive 'six of the best' plus an extended period of having to clean the boys' toilets. They also knew that they would suffer for an undetermined period of time should the culprit not be found.

"You lot can take a quick walk to give the guilty party time to accept the blame and come forward." he shrugged. "If he is not man enough to take his punishment then you will all share it amongst you."

As soon as they were out of earshot a quick conversation soon established that the offender was a boy in grade three and none of the chosen eight. "We can't dob the poor little bugger." said Mobsie, a happy, portly boy who was in grade eight with John and Barry.

"No way." agreed Ginger who was the only representative of grade seven.

"We know that old Guts Ache will keep us all in for weeks if he don't have someone." said Darkie, the youngest of the grade six boys.

Another of the grade six boys added, "It ain't bloody fair, we always cop it. Why doesn't Guts Ache pick on the girls for a change?"

John, worried about the weeks of being kept in, pulled Barry and Ginger aside, "We gotta get home early 'cause Barry's old man is going to sort out the deal on the pennies an' we all got extra work to do for the next month."

Barry saw his mate's point of view. "He'll put it all together and it could be a month before we can play after school again."

John looked at the other group and spoke to his friends. "I reckon the grade six boys will come to a deal; I'll take the cuts if they do the toilet cleaning. I might only get three because of me crook hand."

Ginger nodded "Good idea. But I'll get the cuts. I owe you guys, remember."

"You can't get the cuts Ginge. Old Guts really gives it to you 'cause of that thing with ya old man. No, it's my turn, John, even if ya hand was OK." said Barry.

John knew his mates would offer and as usual it was settled by a contest of rock, paper and scissors which was won or lost, depending on how you looked at it, by Barry.

At this point the deal was put to the others. They agreed, except for Mobsie. "I should have been in the draw for the cuts. I'm not a sook ya know."

"We know ya ain't but the cane seems to hurt you more than others; probably something to do with you being chubby. It's no big deal mate, a couple of Phantom comics will ease the pain."

This answer had helped Mobsie save face but he still added "OK, but I will be in charge of organising the toilet cleaning."

At this the boys trooped back into the room. Barry stepped forward. "It was me Sir, I took old Hazel's bike."

The headmaster's eyes lit up, "Taking the blame on your own are we Hardy? Don't your two mates have the guts to take their share?"

"But I done it on me own, Sir. No one was with me."

"Rubbish boy! You three do everything together. I saw you having your little 'thing' outside to decide who would take it for the group."

Barry spluttered, "We were not playing rock, paper, scissors for that reason Sir we were…."

"Shut up boy!" he thundered. "Not only are you a thief but you are also a liar; while your two friends here are also cowards. If I had the power, I would not have boys the likes of you lot at this school."

At this he walked to the cupboard where he kept his canes, tested two before selecting the third. "Alright Hardy, as you were so keen, you will be the first. Step up boy, don't be shy."

The cane sliced through the air six times for both Barry and Ginger. It was then John's turn.

He was ordered "Good hand first Tiley." When he had received the regulation three on that hand he just stood there wondering what was to happen to the other three.

"Let me look where that cut on your hand is boy." The Head inspected the cut which was on the heel of John's hand. "I do my best work when given a challenge." the class was informed. "Thought you would get off with only three eh? Well think again. Hand up and fingers out straight." The first stroke was perfectly placed catching the fingers and the tip of the thumb but missing the actual palm. Feeling very pleased with himself the Head took less time with the second swing and this one caught the palm just off the stitched area.

"Jesus Christ!" screamed John dropping to one knee and clutching his hand.

"How dare you blaspheme in front of me! Stand up, the cane never went near the cut on your hand. As I said, Tiley, you are a coward and because you are I won't embarrass you any more by giving you the last of your six."

Almost immediately following the administering of the punishment the classes were interrupted by Miss Berry, teacher for the lower half of the school. With her was a very frightened boy who she had just overheard telling his friend about taking Hazel's bike to the shop.

If Mister Golding felt any remorse over the boys being wrongly punished, he certainly never let on to the recipients. The toilet duty was cancelled and that was the end of it. He probably justified his actions by the fact that Barry had admitted to taking the bike. However at least the trio were out of school at three thirty along with the rest of the children, "How's the hand mate?" asked Ginger as they walked down the school steps.

"Hurting like a dog with a glass bottle bait." came the reply "Soon as we get away a bit I'll have a bit of a deco at it."

"Reckon ya should dob to ya Mum. She'll sort ol' Goldie out."

"Aw ya can't tell with grown-ups; probably better off to say I banged it playing. At least that way I am sure that I won't get in any more strife."

Here Barry joined the conversation. "Yup! It has been a pretty rough couple of days. Just hope our luck is about to change. The old man coulda sold the pennies for more than a tenner, ya never know."

As the boys walked towards the Hardy house John removed the layers of blood-encrusted bandage off his hand: they stopped as the last piece of gauze was peeled off.

"Bloody hell mate, no wonder ya squealed. He damn well busted 'er wide open."

Inspection of the damaged hand revealed that the force of the cane had torn out all the stitches. The wound looked a mess but, from past experience, John knew that he would heal quickly as long as he kept it reasonably clean.

"Do ya reckon I might get another bandage at your place Baz. This one has had the Richard that's for sure."

"No worries mate. Mum'll fix 'er up - probably cut them stitches out 'cause they ain't doin nothin'."

"Beauty. That way it'll be a couple a days before my Mum will see it, an' by then she'll be jake. Teachers should be made t' get the cuts when they do something wrong, fair dinkum no wonder some kids play the wag."

His mate looked at him "I've never played the wag mate, have you."

John thought for a while before answering his friend, "Year I did once when we lived in a place called Ballon, I tell ya cobber that is the worst town in the world." He paused as his mind went back to the only time in his young life when he wasn't happy, "yep I had a blue with the headmasters son 'n I knew I was gunna cop it the next day."

He stopped suddenly and lifted one foot, "dam, I got a Christ thorn in me hoof, have ya got your pocket knife so I can have a bit of a dig at her."

Barry handed his knife to John who sat down on the road and commenced to dig away at the thorn imbedded in his foot. "So what happened when ya played the wag," his mate asked.

While he dug at his foot John continued "I had this mate Butch 'n he use ta wag it all the time so the next morning I went bush with him. But I'm not a lucky bloke ya know 'cause we hid our school bags so we could get around and go for a swim ya know. Well this was ok until we reckoned it was time t' head home 'n do ya reckon we could find where we hid 'm, we searched high 'n low, by the time we found the dam bags I reckoned it was pretty late." At this point he gave a sigh of relief as he pulled the quarter inch of Christ thorn out of his foot, "good as new" he said testing his foot on the ground.

Folding the knife he returned it to its owner who immediately asked "come on cobber wot happened ya gotta tell me."

John continued as they walked on, "well once I found me bag I took off for the camp where we lived, I tell ya mate I was sure me mum would have asked other kids why I was late 'n I thought someone would open their yap for sure. Well I raced in 'n Mum asked, wot the hell I was doin' home at this time, I started t' tell he I was kept in at school, 'n she said look at the clock. I tell ya mate I nearly fell off me perch, it was only two thirty, I was home an hour early."

By this time they had arrived and Barry never got to know of the trouble John got into for playing the wag. They could however hear Clarrie and his wife talking out on the back verandah. "Come out here boys. I got a bit of news for ya."

No second invitation was required and they could hardly contain themselves as they stood patiently while Clarrie took his time about finishing his cup of tea.

"Seen that bloke I was telling ya about." he said enjoying the look on the boys' faces. "Yep, he loved them pennies. Reckons they are as good as ya can get these days." Thrusting his hand into his pocket he pulled out a ten pound note and handed it to his son. "There ya go boys, best deal I could for ya."

All three thanked the big man but could not hide their disappointment at the payment being at the low end of the scale that had been discussed.

Later, after Mrs Hardy had cleaned up and dressed John's hand, they were again going over their finances sitting on the floor in Barry's room.

"Even with this tenner and all our savings we are still short a couple of quid of what we have to pay old man Newton." said Barry, disappointed that his Dad had not got a better price for the coins. "Gee I really thought we were gonna be sittin' pretty."

"Look mate, ya old man sold them in one day, an' he got a good price. Heck! My Dad wouldn't have been able to help, so I am happy with what we got. It's a lot more than we had before."

Ginger agreed. "We can get the rest of the money. Might take a while but we'll get it, no sweat."

At this point they looked to find Clarrie Hardy standing at the door. "Oh I'm sorry boys there was something I forgot to tell you. That ten quid is the final payment on those coins. Yep, the bloke that bought em reckons that you lot had already picked up his deposit when ya nicked that 'old brass wheel.'

CHAPTER SIX

THEM BOOTS

The boys looked gloomily at the box of dog-eared comics on the floor before them.

"Musta read 'em all a hundred times," said John, giving the carton a nudge with his foot.

"I reckon there must be some kind of thing that says it's gotta rain on the weekend," he concluded with an exaggerated sigh. His red-headed mate, Ginger, agreed. "This rain has been comin' for a while, mate but it cudda waited a couple more days I reckon."

"It's Sundy t'day 'n I'll betcha by school tomorra the rain will be gone 'n we'll be sitting in school on a beautiful sunny day." Another sigh. "It's not blooming fair."

The two discussed the unfairness of weekend rain and the possibility of making a dash down the street to Skimmy Campbell's place in the hope he would swap some of the comics in the box. "Skimmy's pretty picky about wot he swaps ya know; his comics always have the covers on 'n no pages loose or missin'."

"Yep, I know," replied John. "And the last time I went there he didn't want any of mine, so it would probably be a bit of a waste goin' up t' see him…. although his Mum makes great milo drinks and usually asks if we want one." At this point in the conversation a vehicle pulled up in front of the house; John recognised it as one of only two four-wheel drives in town and it belonged to the station master, Charles Gibson.

The two occupants got out and made a dash for the verandah where the boys were sitting. They both wiped their boots on the sugar bag put there for just that reason and the driver slapped his sodden hat against his leg. "Afternoon boys! Good weather for ducks eh?" John replied to both men at the same time, "G'day Mister Gibson, Mister RoEdwards, I reckon ya must be looking for Dad." Heck RoEdwards replied, "Nailed it in one Blondie; can ya give him a shout please?"

This was unnecessary as Arthur had heard their arrival and came out to meet them. "Come through to the kitchen," he invited. "Isobel has just made a brew." Both men looked down at their muddy boots but Arthur waved aside their concerns. "Not a problem; you have taken the worst off." The two visitors then tossed their hats onto the verandah and followed Arthur through to the kitchen at the rear of the house.

"Wot do ya reckon is goin' on?" asked the little red-head in a hushed voice. John thought for a while then replied, "Must be Ambulance stuff, 'cause sometimes if its rainin' or they gotta go in the bush, Mister Gibson takes his Land Rover. I know Mister Macky is away 'n Mum and Dad are hoIsobelry ambulance bearers so I betcha one of 'em will be goin' out to an accident or something."

"Are we gunna go to Skimmy's place?" John was asked.

"Nah." he replied. "Let's stick around here 'n find out wot's goin' on."

"Sorry. I got some stuff to do at home but I might go to Skimmy's first 'n have a deco at what he's got. Can I take a few of yours, just in case?"

John bent down and leafed through the comics in the box. "Go for your life, mate. He likes those little war ones, you know, Battle of Britain that sort of thing; also any Walt Disney in good nick." Together the boys selected a handful that they thought might tempt Skimmy into a swap. Ginger shoved these under his shirt and with a quick "See ya later, mate!" took off up the street towards Skimmy's house.

John now had to put himself in a position to be able to listen in to what was being discussed. To do this he went around the verandah to his bedroom door but as soon as he was inside his father called him into the kitchen.

"Has Ginger gone home?" he was asked.

"Yep, he went to Skimmy's place to see if he could swap some comics. I don't think he will be back as he told me he had some jobs to do at home for his old man."

Arthur nodded "That's OK because I need you to come for a bit of a drive with me." The thought of a boring afternoon immediately disappeared from John's mind. "Beauty," he said with huge grin. "Where we gunna go?"

"Going to go," corrected his mother.

John repeated "going to go" before his father continued. "Do you remember old Mister Triffet - the foreman out on Sunny Plain? He gave us a bit of a hand the day we ran the line for the new bore drain out there."

"He gave me that beaut belt buckle didn't he? 'Course I remember him."

"Well, it appears that he had a bit of a blue with the new manager; did his block, packed his swag, grabbed a horse and rode off intending to come into town." John was wondering where a drive with his father fitted into this and asked, "Do ya reckon he's got tossed or something if he hasn't got to town by now?"

Arthur nodded at his son's assessment. "He set off on Friday night and even with this bad weather coming on he should have been at his sister's place here in town by late Saturday afternoon. Apparently the manager rang early this morning to ask him to reconsider and come back."

After this short summary the two visitors stood up to leave. Charles Gibson turned to Isobel, "Thanks for the cuppa, Isobel. Arthur, we'll get the stuff from the ambulance station plus maybe a bit of medicine from the pub," he concluded with a wink.

Arthur talked as he walked with the two men to the front door "As discussed, I'll get Isobel to make a bit of tucker we can take with us. John, get the chains for my truck, a good tow rope, a couple of smalls tarps and make sure the forty-four on the back is full of petrol." The local butcher, Heck Thompson, asked "What time are we going to meet and where?"

"The sooner the better." Arthur answered. "It would be nice to be at the turn-off to Sunny before dark; so let's be at the end of the bitumen near the cemetery by two thirty; that gives us just over half an hour." Both men agreed and as Heck pulled on his hat he said, "We'll drop in at the police station and let the Sarge know we are set to go. Oh, by the way, when are you going to fit the chains?"

"Certainly before we are off the bitumen, that's for sure." replied Arthur.

"Do you reckon you and young John will be able to manage to put 'em on?"

"We'll be OK. John has helped me with them a few times so I don't see any problems. So, at the cemetery around two-thirty." Arthur added as the other two dashed to their vehicle.

John was still unsure of what he and his father were going to do but in his mind he had already decided that it was going to be a 'life and death' mission. "Wot are we gunna do, Dad?" he asked as soon as his father returned to the kitchen. "What are we going to do?" corrected Isobel. "Sometimes I think you are speaking another language."

John again copied her but looked to his father for an answer. "Well, Mister RoEdwards and Mister Gibson will take his four-wheel drive and I will take the work truck which should be OK with chains on the rear wheels. We will search from the town to the station turn off and the station people will look along the road to the homestead."

John's face fell as there was no mention of what role he was to play, which, after all was what he was asking about. His father noticed this but left him wondering just a little bit longer. "From the information from Sunny Plains, the Sarge is pretty sure that old Triffet went across country and if he did have an accident, if he was able, he would have walked to the nearest road."

By now they were in the truck and heading to the Council depot to collect more equipment. "But what if he's hurt too bad to walk?" asked John.

"Well, the Sarge is organising a group that is going to do a horseback search at first light tomorrow if we don't find him today." John was still unsure that he was actually going and not merely helping his father to pick up the gear that was needed but he cheerfully helped him load up the chains, tarps, tow rope and a couple of pieces of master matting just for 'insurance' his father told him.

All loaded they returned to the house where Isobel had thermos flasks of tea and coffee and a pile of sandwiches ready, as well as wet weather gear and spare clothing for Arthur. As they got this organised to take out to the truck, she said to John, "Well, if you are going with your father get your rain coat, put some boots on and get a spare set of dry clothes; also get a jumper but not your blue one as I know you around mud."

John was off like a scalded cat, gathering from his mother's voice that she was not too pleased that he was going and he didn't want to give anyone any chance to review the decision. The truth of the decision was that all had agreed that at worst the boy might spend a night in the truck and that his young eyes would definitely be an asset to the party.

John put his gear with the pile on the verandah which now included some blankets and their personal first-aid kit. Isobel saw that Arthur was about to question the inclusion of the family first-aid kit so she cut him off, "I know Charles and Heck will have one from the ambulance station but I keep this one stocked and you can be sure there is everything in there that you could need." Arthur agreed with her adding "You are right. Sometimes the station kits are not refilled when they return from a callout."

By now John had everything stowed in his father's Dodge truck, either behind the front seat or on it between them and with a "See you later!" to Isobel they took the town's only bitumen road to where it ended at the town cemetery. The others had not arrived and as the rain had eased for the moment, Arthur and John set about fitting the mud chains to the vehicle's rear dual wheels. This was a task John had been involved in on a number of occasions and he knew the drill well.

As he threw them off the back of the truck his father said, "We'll put the new chains on the outside tyres as the old ones will be easier to fit to the inside ones." John sorted them as asked then said "Are we gunna lay 'em out together and try to get them on in one go?"

"No: inside first then the outside, same as we did last time." was the reply.

The last of the chains were just being finished when the rain returned and the Land Rover arrived. "Sorry we're late Arthur but we waited at the police station to get the latest news from Sunny Plains, and there is still no sign of George. Apparently, it is really chucking it down out there." said Heck RoEdwards. Charles Gibson added, "Tell Arthur what the manager of Sunny told the Sarge." Heck gave a bit of a laugh. "Charles's cranky because the manager said he wasn't coming out to the turn off as he couldn't see the point."

Arthur showed his annoyance with this news but before he could say anything Charles held up his hands as if in surrender. "I know what you're thinking Arthur, the only point that bloke needs is the one on the end of my boot up his rear end. The bloody fool does not realise that if on foot, George would have two choices. One would be to his left and hit the station road and the other would be straight ahead to the main road." Pausing for a bit Charles then added, "I reckon because he knows the country so well even at night and perhaps injured, he would know exactly where he was and pick the easiest and quickest option to go to where he knew he was most likely to be found."

"Well." said Arthur. "Our part of the search has been set out by the Sarge. We are to go to the turn off and then return to town. As far as I am concerned that is exactly what we should do." The other two men agreed and at that everybody got into their respective vehicles and headed off. As previously agreed, Arthur would lead as his truck was more likely to get bogged. At which point the Land Rover would be in a better position to pull them backwards onto solid ground.

A couple of vehicles had already been along the road since the rain had started so the road had been chopped up which made the going harder, with Arthur having to use all his skill to keep the truck on the crest of the road and out of the table drain. The rain was making it difficult to see because the wipers were not able to keep up with the deluge.

"Even if we aren't yet in the area where it is possible for him to be, you never know: Sunny Plains is on your side, John, so keep your eyes peeled in that direction. Look for anything out of the ordinary and don't be afraid to give a shout. I would rather stop a dozen times for nothing than miss him. Also keep a bit of an eye on the blokes behind us as they could get into strife just as easily as we can even if they do have four-wheel drive."

John nodded and strained his eyes looking through the rain and looking back occasionally to be sure that they were still being followed. The rain eased a little, improving John's visibility but the road surface continued to worsen and the chains on the rear duals were now clogged with mud which did not have the grip they had had earlier. "I think at the turn-off into Walkers' place I'll stop, get rid of some of the mud and give the chains a bit of a clean," Arthur told his son. "Yea! I can feel her losing her grip every now and again, although we are doin' better than the others as they are all over the place like a chicken with its head cut off."

Arthur tried to get a look at the Land Rover in his side mirror, watched them for a few seconds then said, "Our problem is we have been going almost two hours and with the turn off to Walkers' just up here, it means that we are doing less then ten miles an hour. At this rate it will be dark long before we get to the turn-around point at the Sunny Plains road."

Giving the following vehicle plenty of warning of his intention to stop, Arthur came to a halt just past the turn off. John was out immediately, grabbing one of the trenching shovels from behind the seat and getting to work cleaning the mud from between the duals and as much as he could off the chains. Arthur walked back to the other vehicle. "Bloody tough going." he remarked.

"Bloody oath." said Charles Gibson, "This has convinced me that I need to get a set of chains for this baby, these lug-tread tyres are OK but I reckon with chains on, this would be a piece of cake." As the men chatted John called from under his father's truck, "I reckon I can hear another vehicle coming." The men stopped talking then agreed there was definitely the sound of an engine coming towards them.

Having finished his cleaning job, John slid from under the Dodge and climbed onto the back, "It's not a car," he shouted as the rain started to fall heavily again, "Could be a truck but I reckon it's a tractor." His guess proved to be correct as, five minutes later, a very muddy Ferguson from Walkers' Bend pulled onto the road behind the Land Rover.

Leaving the machine running, the driver kicked on the brake lock with his boot and then jumped down. Frank 'Mitch' Mitchell was the sort of young bloke who was never without a grin, a good word and a helping hand to whoever needed it. He wasn't a big lad but he made up for his lack of physical stature by his drive and enthusiasm. His late grandfather, Len Walker, had taken up the property, now known as Walkers' Bend, around 1910. It had been a tough first four years but he had been getting things established when World War I broke out. Three months later he shipped out for Gallipoli and later for the Western Front.

During his absence, Walkers' Bend was run by his wife, Jennifer, and a twelve year old jackaroo named Tod Mitchell. Four years later, on his daughter's ninth birthday, Len returned to Walkers' Bend just in time to see Tod depart. His return was a mixture of happiness and sadness as he had spent the last three months in hospital in England recovering from an explosion which had blown off his right hand and blinded him in his right eye. The returning digger never thought of his loss as a disability but more of an inconvenience. Young Tod's return a year later found Walkers' Bend flourishing. Len's daughter finally married Tod after she had been away for some years in the big smoke but it was ten years before their marriage was blessed with a son who was to be their only child and Len's only grandson. If there was ever a chip off the old block it was Mitch.

"G'day Arthur, Charles, Heck and, stone-the-bloody-crows, Blondie's here as well! How are ya, mate?" John had known Mitch since he was going and coming from boarding school and therefore had always called him by his first name. "Great thanks Mitch, wot cha doin' here?"

"Dad heard that you blokes were gunna look along the road for ol' George from Sunny so we decided t' give ya a hand. The Fergie is pretty good in the mud so here I am."

Arthur thanked the young man for his concern and all agreed that another vehicle and pair of eyes would be a big help. Especially as, once they were using lights, the extra swivel ones mounted on the mud-guards of the tractor would be very handy for searching the edges of the road. The small mismatched convoy started off and the driving rain returned. They were now in an area where George might have reached the road, so all eyes were focused on the direction he would have been coming from.

A couple of hours later as the sun started to disappear, Arthur called another stop. "Get Mitch to join us in the back of the Land Rover for a brew." he asked his son. He grabbed the thermos flasks, one pack of sandwiches and a packet of Monty Carlo biscuits and went back to the other vehicle, to be joined almost immediately by Mitch and John. John poured the steaming hot tea into battered old pannikins, handed these around to the group and made a very milky sweet one for himself.

"How long to the Sunny Plains turn off?" asked Heck.

"At the rate we are going I would say about an hour and a half. What do you think Mitch?" said Arthur. Young Mitch pushed his sodden hat back on his head and took a slurp of his tea "That grid a couple of miles back is twenty miles from our road so the Sunny turn off is about fifteen miles away. Your hour and a half would be about right."

Charles threw the dregs of his tea out of the window, took the last Monty Carlo that John had been eyeing and said, "Between one and a half and two hours puts us well in the dark before we turn around so let's hit the road."

The tractor now took the lead so that everyone would be able to take advantage of the visibility from the swivel lights as darkness fell. Over two hours later they finally reached the Sunny Plains turn off and by now everybody was starting to feel the strain plus the disappointment of not locating 'old George.'

Despite having wet weather gear on, everyone was a little on the damp side, especially Mitch who was soaked to the skin. When they had turned the vehicles around for the return trip Arthur asked the group, "What say we take half an hour, light a fire, get dried out a bit and have another cuppa and a bit to eat?" All agreed, with Heck saying, "Bloody good idea Arthur. Half an hour is neither here nor there now that the sun has gone and while young Mitch here is as wet as a shag on a rock, we are all a bit damp from having the windows down."

Quickly a pile of very wet wood was gathered in the middle of the road, half a tin of kerosene was taken out of one of the lamps and an equal amount of petrol was mixed with it. This was poured around the base and immediately a match was thrown onto the damp area. It went off with a great 'wooff' and five minutes later everyone was warming themselves around a roaring blaze.

With warmth returning to his limbs, Mitch announced "Even in this weather I reckon ol' George will be able to see the fire from miles away, 'n I wouldn't be surprised if he just appeared and said, "How ya goin'?"

"Aside from this search, I hear you had one out at the cemetery the other day Arthur? What was that about," asked Heck. Huddled against the wind Arthur took a final drag on his cigarette before throwing the but into the fire. "Old bloke that was working for me a couple of years ago, died on one of the road gangs. We couldn't find any next of kin, we knew his name and that he was a pom. So we buried him and sent the details to the British Embassy." Arthur paused and lit another cigarette before continuing "couple of weeks ago we get a letter saying the bloke was Lord so and so and the family wanted his body returned to England to burry in the family plot."

"Fair dinkum, get out your pullin' me leg" Heck came back.

"Well I tell you we went out dug him up, put what was left in the special box they sent and sent him off. Well I think we sent the right bloke," he finished with a laugh.

However, despite their beacon there was no sign of George and they headed back towards town. "Still keep an eye out." said Arthur, "You never know, he might have made it nearer to the road since we passed."

Within ten minutes of the party leaving their makeshift camp the wind and rain returned with a vengeance and the condition of the road got worse and worse, with their progress being reduced almost to a walking pace. Suddenly, without warning, the lights on the tractor went off completely. The convoy stopped and, using a torch and hurricane lamp, the men tried to see if there was anything obviously wrong. The driving rain and wind made this task impossible and realizing this, Charles asked Mitch, "If we put you as the middle vehicle will you be all right?"

"Yar, I'll be jake with one behind and one in front." came the immediate reply.

As the vehicles were being repositioned, John said to his father "Dad, I know this sounds stupid but I just saw a red light on this side of the road." His father raised his eyebrows, "Could be a min min light." he said jokingly. "That's not the side George will be on, you know that." John didn't reply but continued to stare off into the darkness, perhaps hoping to see the legendary min min light.

A moment later he grabbed his father's arm, "There it is again Dad. This time it gave one short flash and one long one." Arthur's eye followed his son's pointing finger and almost immediately saw the flash of red that John was speaking of. "There Dad! Did you see it that time?" he asked excitedly.

"Yes. I saw what you saw, son but I haven't a damn clue what it is." Keeping his eye on the spot he got out of the truck and went to the others explaining what he and John had just seen. "There it is again!" said Mitch.

"Yep! I definitely saw it that time." said Charles and Heck together.

"Do ya reckon it's a min min?" asked John wiping the rain from his face.

"I believe in the min min, Blondie," replied Heck, "but I have never heard of anyone seeing one when it's raining."

Mitch looked again and said to John, "It looks a long way off, but if we walk out of the glow of everyone's headlights we might be able to guess what it is and how far away it is."

John turned to his father who immediately nodded his consent." Take the lantern and do not go anywhere that you can't see our headlights."

"You don't have to worry about that Dad; you can bet your boots I'm not gunna get lost out there, that's for sure." With the extent of their travel settled, John and Mitch waited for another flash from the red light. When it came it seemed further away or fainter and just flashed the once. They sloshed their way through the table drain and set off in the direction they had last seen the mystery light. Only fifty yards into their search it appeared again, to their left: it seemed close and at ground level.

Above the noise of the rain and their clumping boots John heard, "Are you blokes bloody stupid?" He pulled Mitch to a stop and asked, "Did you hear that?"

"I thought I heard something that sounded like a voice but I'm not sure."

"Damn spooky I reckon." said John. "Do min min lights talk to ya?"

Mitch was about to answer when, clear as a bell, they both heard "I'm just here ya pair of bloody old women!" Holding up the hurricane lamp they saw not ten paces from them a sheet of old galvanised iron with a hand waving to them from underneath. "Wot the bloody hell?" exclaimed Mitch. John pulled the sheet away. "That was the last drag of me fag," the voice said.

"It's Mister Triffet!" yelled John "We've found him!" Mitch knelt beside the man but a quick look told him that the bloke was not in good shape. He put his hand on George's shoulder. "You'll be right now ol' mate." Then to John, "We can't move him so go and get the others."

Making a bee-line for the lights John charged through the storm drain shouting, "It's him! He's there!. We've found him!. He looks a bit crook but he can talk." His father put both hands on his son's shoulders and said "Whoa! Slow down, son. What the hell are you shouting about?"

John took a breath and told them. "It's Mister Triffet. He doesn't look good, especially his leg."

Arthur grabbed the first-aid kit and asked, "Can you blokes bring the stretcher, blankets and maybe that small tarp?" Not waiting for an answer he was off leaving Charles, Heck and John to bring the rest of the stuff.

The idea of taking a vehicle to the patient was not even considered as all knew that none of them would get through the table drain. As they were just about to leave the vehicles, for some unknown reason, the lights on the tractor decided to work again. "Well, I'll be a monkey's uncle!" said Heck as he swiveled the light so that their path and the area where Arthur and Mitch were, was well illuminated. "That'll make it easier for Arthur to get a good deco at ol' George."

By the time they arrived Arthur's examination had revealed a compound break of his left leg. "How far have you come on that leg, George?"

"Got thrown Saturday arvo 'n found a stick to shove under me arm, missed the road 'cause I was a bit wonky, 'n this bloody rain didn't help. I stepped onto me sheet of tin 'n then got under it; then, 'cause me leg's a bit crook, I musta slept most of t'day."

"By the look of the blood around the top of your boot, it looks like a compound fracture."

"Course it's a bloody compound break ya bloody nong, even I know that; every step I took felt like a sword was being shoved up through me leg."

"OK" said Arthur. "The first step is to get him back to the road where I will decide what has to be done to make him comfortable for the trip into town."

The fold-out stretcher was placed next to the man and with Arthur supporting the injured leg he was moved onto it. Arthur said later that he could feel the broken bones moving, but the man never even murmured. With one of the men on each corner of the stretcher and John leading with the lamp, the trip back to the road was uneventful. One of the drop-sides on Arthur's truck was lowered and George was put straight into the back. The light on the tractor now gave Arthur a chance to get a proper look at the broken leg from a first-aid point of view.

"What do you reckon Arthur?" Heck asked.

In a low voice he replied "It's not good and I am worried about circulation to his foot. I can tell you no matter how slow we go, the trip back to town is going to be murder for the poor bugger."

"Hey Arthur," said George "I have been crawling and hopping with this bloody leg for over a day, so don't whisper: say wot ya gotta say so I can hear ya."

"Sorry George, you're right. I am worried about the blood flow to your foot past the break and also immobilising the leg for the trip back to town."

"How are ya gunna check the blood in me foot?"

"I will have to cut your boot off, mate as the pain while I'm getting it off the regular way would probably kill you."

The reply to this was immediate and definitely final. "Pain I can live with but I can tell ya now no one is gunna cut up them boots." Arthur started to talk but the old man cut him off. "I won them boots in a card game; married the only woman I ever loved in em, 'n I buried her and our son in them. No! I don't care, nothin'. Them boots don't get cut, ya understand?" Arthur held up his hands in surrender, "OK, mate, I'll leave the boot removal for the hospital where they can give you something decent for the pain." Then to the others he asked, "Can you guys give me a hand as I want to splint the two legs together then wrap enough around both legs and the stretcher in the hope it will reduce his movement during the trip."

The law of the day allowed ambulance bearers to administer only two fairly low-level pain killers and Arthur decided it was now time to give George the two he carried in the first-aid kit. The rain made things awkward but the men soon readied their patient for the ordeal to come.

"What about the blood flow to his foot that had you worried, Arthur?" Mitch asked.

"Not much I can do about that. Even if I did find something was wrong, I am not sure there is anything I could do about it, so we just have to hope the couple of hours to town isn't the difference between losing and keeping his foot."

Both Heck and Charles nodded their agreement and Heck said "I think the back of the truck is the best place for him to travel, we can tie the stretcher down and have the bigger tarp coming off the fuel drum to keep him a bit drier. The back of the Land Rover, while dry, doesn't have enough room without either his head or feet hanging over the tail gate." John got the other tarp and ropes from behind the front seat and he and

Mitch tied it behind the forty-four gallon drum and down to the tail-gate, forming a little tent.

While they were doing this the others tied the stretcher securely to the truck. This done, Charles handed the stockman the bottle of OP rum he had purchased before leaving town. "I know you shouldn't have alcohol at a time like this, especially after those tablets Arthur gave ya."

George snatched the bottle of OP from Charles's hand. "You bastard Gibson you been holding out on me. This is the real McCoy and I sure as hell cudda used some before Doc Arthur here went to work on me leg." Charles laughed as George cracked the seal of the bottle removed the cap and gulped down the potent rum. He sighed and wiped his mouth on this sleeve. "Bloody mother's milk," he said before taking another large pull at the bottle. "And Gibson I forgive ya, mate."

By the time they were ready to leave about half the bottle of OP rum was gone and George wasn't feeling a lot of pain at all; as a matter of fact he wasn't feeling a lot of anything. He was well wrapped in blankets and tarps and even though it was still raining quite heavily it looked like the stockman's journey to town would be a relatively comfortable one.

After a final inspection of his patient Arthur gave him the bad news. "Another nip and that's it for the rum, George."

"Wot are ya talking about? I'll need it for the trip t' town."

"Sorry mate. If I deliver you to the hospital drunk they may not be able to go to work on that leg of yours." At that he quickly pulled the bottle from George's hand. The OP was definitely taking effect as he slurred slightly. "You're a bigger bastard then that bastard Gibson."

Unmoved Arthur called John to the back of the truck. "I want you to ride in the back with Mister Triffet. I need to know how he is going and, as the sides are up, no one will be able to see him, so I know it will be a bit rough but it looks like your it."

"I'll be jake" said John. "I got me jumper 'n I can get under the tarp a bit as well."

"If you think anything is wrong bang on the roof immediately." The boy was told in his father's very serious voice. At that the vehicles moved off, "Ya feel OK Mister Triffet?" asked John as soon as they were under way. With a slightly lopsided grin came the reply, "No worries Blondie, but that bottle of OP ya old man took away wudda made me a whole lot better, that's for sure."

"Dad's a qualified ambulance man ya know 'n he knows a lot about medical stuff."

"Maybe, but he don't know anything about medical goodness in OP rum." At that he held up his hand, "See that scar?" he asked.

"Holy mackerel!" said John on seeing the huge inch wide scar that ran from the man's wrist to the base of his index finger. "Wot happened to ya hand?"

"Bloody mad steer pinned me to a yard post; but me point is, that after a bottle of OP the station cook cleaned it out and stitched her up good as new. Mind you he also had a bottle to 'steady his hand' or so he said."

"Boy! I betcha that hurt like billy-oh."

"Never felt a thing Blondie. I tell ya the ol' OP's the best thing goin'."

The rain had almost stopped so John pulled the tarp from around the fuel drum so that they could both get some fresh air. The hurricane lamp immediately blew out but the torch was still working so the loss of the lamp wasn't a problem.

John sat at the old man's head so he could be heard easily above the noise of the three vehicles grinding their way through the mud. "Ya know what Mister Triffet?"

"Wot Blondie? Wot do ya know?"

"Well I reckon if the lights on the tractor hadna' gorn out just when they did I would never have seen the glow from ya cigarette. Being stopped 'n no light comin' from the mudguard lights on the tractor, I could see into the dark pretty good."

The old man pondered this for a while then replied, "I reckon it was me missus looking out for me. Before she died she said I would never be alone 'n she would keep an eye on me. She did it before a couple a times, so I betta thank her again I reckon."

Before John could enquire as to what the old man meant, his father stopped the truck. Wondering what was going on, John went to his father's window. "How is it going son?" he asked.

"Pretty good Dad. Mister Triffet had a bit of a sleep but I reckon it was from the OP stuff. He's awake now 'n talkin' OK." But before he could ask why they had stopped he got his answer as Mitch walked up.

"I reckon you'll be right from here to town, so I'll see ya later Arthur, 'n you too Blondie."

"Thanks a lot Mitch I'll give you a bell when we get to town."

"Good-oh Arthur." Then finally, "Hang in there, George. The hospital will get ya sorted, no worries."

As Mitch returned to the tractor, Arthur relit the lamp and checked on his patient. The man was now very pale and slipping in and out of consciousness. Arthur was unsure if this was from fatigue, the OP rum or a medical reason.

As he was checking, he was joined by Charles and Heck who could see that Arthur was worried. "I reckon we could step on it a bit now that the tractor has gone," Heck said, nodding towards George. Charles agreed. "Yep. He don't look so good at all." At that moment George spoke for the first time since they had stopped. "Wot would ya know ya bastard, Gibson? If ya hadda given me the OP straight away I wouldda been right as rain by now." He finished with another "Ya bastard." before he slipped into unconsciousness again.

Let's get going while he's out," said Arthur. "John, you can come up in the front with me if you want to get warm."

"Nah, I'll stay with Mister Triffet just to make sure." replied his son.

Without the tractor, the two vehicles made good time for the remaining twelve miles or so. George's muttering and groaning was worrying for John and the first sign of the town lights was a great relief to the young Tiley. The sound of the chains clattering on the bitumen was music to his ears and five minutes later they pulled up in front of the hospital.

Isobel must have been watching for their lights, as she arrived there almost at the same time as they did. She spoke briefly to Arthur then called to John, "Come on mate. It's a hot bath, a feed and off to bed for you."

Later while eating some hot stew, John asked his mother, "Mum, Mister Triffet reckoned his dead wife was looking out for him. What did he mean by that?" His mother started to explain but her son's head slowly dropped to his chest almost falling into his stew.

The local doctor stabilised George that night and removed his boot without cutting it. The next day, which as John had predicted, was hot and sunny, the flying doctor picked George up and transported him to the coast where surgeons were able to save his leg.

A couple of months later he called in on the Tileys on his way back to Sunny Plains. "You blokes are good people," he said. "Just like my wife; she was good people, 'n that's the only thing wot's important, except for 'them boots'."

> The old man knew that his time was near,
> Yet his weathered face, it held no fear
> Of what was beyond this mortal coil
> Or what had passed in his life of toil.
>
> A trembling hand reached for his boots;
> The tools of his trade, that told of his roots.
> His feet rejoiced at their firm embrace
> And this was written in the old man's face.
>
> His mind went back and remembered when
> Him and them boots became best friends
> The pot was his, fair and square
> Yep! He'd won them boots with a single pair.
>
> He wore them boots on the day he wed,
> The woman who was his world, he said.
> And when she passed, giving birth to a son
> He prayed by their grave with them boots on.
>
> An' when he got thrown in the drivin' rain
> Them boots had eased the terrible pain
> Of a break so bad that the doctor said,
> "It's a miracle mate, ya should be dead."
>
> And now he lay back on the bed awhile,
> Heard their voices and had to smile,
> As they poked and prodded and tried in vain
> To kindle the spark of life again.
>
> At last they let the old man rest
> Folded his hands on his now still chest.

He had not moved for near ten days
Since a stroke had stopped his wandering ways.

The mystery now was how it could be
That a man in condition such as he
Could again pull them boots into place
And pass from this world with a smile on his face.

By *John Tiley*

CHAPTER SEVEN

THE DUNNYMAN'S DAUGHTER

The summer passed slowly and it was about this time that the family went through an event that was to stay with them for the rest of their lives and this was especially so in John's case. Perhaps it is better that this story is told by him.

I jumped the three steps to the front verandah almost landing on top of a young girl sitting on the floor reading one of my comics. My unheralded entrance startled her to the extent that she dropped the 'Phantom' and shuffled quickly across the floor on her backside. There she cringed, hard against the opposite wall looking as though she had been caught in the middle of some terrible act.

"I… I… I… was just reading it," she stammered.

Almost as surprised as she was, I asked, "Wotcha doin' here?"

"Waiting for me Dad. He is talking t' your Dad about a job."

I picked up the comic from where she had let it drop and handed it back to her, "Do ya have any comics to swap? 'Cause I've got heaps if ya have!"

She looked down and shook her head, at the same time she found the place she was reading before I had interrupted her. It appeared that our conversation was over. This relieved me somewhat as my mate, Ginger, was coming over and I had to arrange some food before we headed off to the creek for a swim.

My father was the works manager or overseer for the Shire and it was not unusual for him to hold interviews or impromptu meetings on a Saturday. Sitting at the kitchen table talking to him was a tall dark skinned man with slightly oriental features. He had obviously not shaved for a while and his jet-black hair was almost collar length. His whole appearance immediately reminded me of a pirate captain who had died at the hands of Errol Flynn in his latest swash-buckling thriller.

"John, this is Mister Wodomo."

"Pleased t' meet ya," I said, offering my hand but not game to try to pronounce his name.

"Likewise, but forget the mister and call me Tex." He said with a slight knowing smile.

I looked at my father who explained to Tex; "We prefer the boys not to call adults by their first name. Don't worry he'll soon get to pronounce Wodomo properly."

I left the men to carry on their discussions and went to the business end of the kitchen where my mother was busy making a brew of tea and had scones ready to go in the oven.

"Can I make a sanga for me and Ginger?"

Mum replied exactly as I knew she would; "Doesn't that boy ever eat at home? Also, how many times do I have to tell you it's, Ginger and I?"

Mum's bark was worse than her bite and I knew she was actually very fond of my little redheaded mate.

"Aw Mum you know what it's like at his place on Saturday arvo."

Probably thinking back on the several occasions when she had involved herself to protect Ginger and his sister from their drunken father, she replied; "Don't cut the slices too thick and use up what is left in the jam tin before you open another".

Mum was bush born and bred and as such was not one for showing emotion. Certainly she was the tougher half of a partnership that was to last over fifty years. She was not a people person and, save for a few years during the war when she had worked for a doctor in Sydney while driving an army *ambulance at night, Mum had pretty much lived in a man's world. Also, having three sons had certainly not improved matters.*

Years later when we started bringing girls home we began to see the feminine side of our mother that had been suppressed during our childhood.

"Why don't you and Ginger ask Molly if she would like to go to the creek? I assume that is where you are going?"

"Who is Molly?" I asked knowing full well who she meant, but stalling for time to enable me to have a good reason to refuse.

"Mister Wodomo's daughter. You must have seen her sitting out front."

"Oh, yes I did see her, but she is reading and I don't reckon she'd want t' come 'cause it's … err … pretty hot for a sheila."

This was not a good answer, as Mum firmly believed that women could hold their own with men in most things; "Absolute rubbish." she said. "Now you go and ask her if she would like a sandwich and a drink of cordial while her Dad has a cup of tea."

Before she could add about asking her to the creek Mister Wodomo saved me.

"Thanks a lot Missus but me an' Arthur are about done. I am gonna take the dunny man job so I reckon me an' Molly better find somewhere we can toss our swags. However, I would like t' ask young John here if he would look out for her at school. The last place we was at the kids give her a bit of stick 'cause of me job."

Having been given a reprieve from having to ask the girl to come to the creek I was more than happy to agree; "She'll be right no worries." I said, quickly going back to making sandwiches.

"Thanks." he nodded. "Her mum was the same about me doin' dunny work. Before Molly came along I could do station work, but because I can't read and write this is the one job that I can get when I live in town so she can go to school."

With that comment he thanked Mum for the offer of tea and stood up to leave. My eyes immediately went to the beautiful sheath knife hanging from his belt. He saw me looking at it and asked; "Do you like knives John?"

A little embarrassed at being caught out I stammered, "Err… yes I sure do, I got a goodun' but that leaves mine for dead."

He quickly unclipped the weapon, flipped it expertly in his hand and passed it to me to look at. I had never seen a knife like this, the handle seemed to be made from a single piece of solid leather while the blade and hand guard were of jet black steel with silver inlays.

"My family on my Dad's side came from Malaya and in that country knife making is a very special trade. This one is me favourite; my Grandfather made it. Although it's mainly for cutting, it throws pretty well."

Now, I considered myself the best knife thrower in town, mainly by virtue of the fact that I could actually get one to stick in to a tree on a regular basis. My brother, Charles, was also pretty good too but as he was away at high school he didn't count. Up to now I had never had an adult express more than a passing interest in knife throwing and therefore was immediately interested in Mr. Wodomo's statement.

"I can throw a knife. The one I've got has a special handle that doesn't break if it don't hit point first." I told him with some pride.

"Well I'm sorry but I can't let ya have a throw of this one, but if it's OK with Arthur I'll show you how."

The look on Mum's face told me that she was not too happy about this but thankfully, Dad nodded his assent, probably interested to see what the new dunnyman could do with his fancy knife. Keen to display my skills I got my own knife from under my mattress; a hiding place that ensured my ability to be able to defend my family from whatever might threaten them during the night. I regularly practiced retrieving and unsheathing it once the lights were out. Sadly on two occasions my mosquito net had suffered as a result of these actions. Even the resulting punishments were not enough deterrent to stop me being ready to take up arms should the situation require it.

Mr. Wodomo balanced my 'bushman's special' in his hand

"Err, I think I'll use me own thanks mate," he said handing it back to me.

The tree in our front yard showed the scars of where I had used my knife as a last line of defense against an advancing enemy. From fifteen to twenty feet I could confidently stick my knife into an area of the trunk that was nominated as the chest. We brothers and our mate often played a game where points were awarded depending on where the knife stuck into the tree. If it fell out before the thrower retrieved it no points were received. A cross about the size of a playing card had been cut into the trunk which was the heart. According to the rules of the game to hit this area meant an instant kill and a win for that round. These were rare and when they did occur they were usually due to the number of attempts rather than skill, although the thrower would never admit to this.

"It's your tree Blondie. Show me how it's done."

At this time my redheaded mate Ginger came through the front gate, he was used to the competitive nature of my family and was therefore not surprised at what he saw.

"G'day Mr. and Mrs. Tiley." he said in his usual chirpy manner. Turning to me he asked, "Wotcha doin' mate?"

I quickly explained what was happening and managed to introduce Ginger to Mister Wodomo without using his name which, by this time, I had forgotten. Even if I had not, I would have definitely made a mess of the pronunciation. I went to a spot where I was at least sure of hitting the tree and having the knife stick in and stay there, so I couldn't help grinning when all went according to plan.

"You throw pretty well, but don't be so tense, just relax and imagine the turns the blade will make to the target. That way you won't over rotate and lose control."

He took his own knife out and I was expecting him to move to where I had thrown, however from a distance almost double mine and in an underhand action he threw. The knife flashed through the air and thudded into the tree about an inch from where the lines of the cross dissected each other. I was amazed, not so much with the intended accuracy, but with the speed and force with which the weapon had been delivered.

"Not so good," he said. "Give us another go will ya?"

His second throw was taken from the same place but he used the more conventional overhand style. This time the blade struck dead centre of the cross, possibly with more force than the first. I moved as if to retrieve the weapon but was waved away. "She's right son I'll get 'er, 'cause she'll be pretty solid." He was right as it took considerable work to get it out of the wood and he did it with a lot of care. Before returning it to its sheath on his belt he wiped the blade and lightly ran his thumb over the tip; I guess checking that there was no damage done.

"Well, I reckon it was a bit of a fluke." said Ginger as we trudged towards the creek.

"I wish I could throw a fluke like that every now and again." I replied remembering how difficult it had been for the man to remove the knife from

the tree trunk. "He told the old man that he likes to hunt wild pigs with a knife: hit 'em just behind the shoulder he said."

"Fair dinkum! I seen a big 'un keep goin' with two 303 bullets in him."

"Seems a pretty quiet sort of a bloke but."

"Maybe, but I wouldn't like to stir him up. I reckon he could probably go a bit with his fists as well. He's got a sorta angry wild look about him."

"He asked me to look out for Molly his daughter at school. He thinks that some kids will tease her 'cause she is the dunnyman's daughter."

"Jeese after seeing her old man throw that bloody knife you wouldn't think anyone would be that stupid."

By this time we had reached the creek and, to our horror, there was already someone swimming in our favourite hole. "Skimmy and a couple of his Convent boarder mates." whispered Ginger, both of us crouching down so as not to be seen.

"Betcha they shouldn't be here 'cause they are swimmin' in the nuddy so not to get their shorts wet."

Ginger looked at me and gave a wicked grin, "Let's pinch their gear an' hide it."

The idea of having two of the usually uniformed and proper Convent school boarders wandering around nude looking for their clothes appealed to me. It would also serve as a reminder to the swimmers that this part of the creek was 'State School' domain and Convent kids should venture here by invitation only. The clothes were in three neat piles quite close to the water's edge however the distance from where we were hidden on top of the creek bank, to the first pile was a good fifty yards.

The question was could we cover that distance before they realised what we were doing and came out of the water to stop us?

"Let's just walk casually down as if we are just going to join them and at the last minute make a dash with their gear." I suggested.

"Ripper idea they will never suspect that we are going to nick their clobber."

We stood up and started down the bank. "G'day Skimmy!" I called "Is the water cold?"

"Bloody oath! Ya comin' in?" came the reply.

"Reckon we might, but how come the Collies are off the leash?"

We called children who boarded at the Convent, boarders hence Boarder Collies or, as on this occasion just Collies. By this time we had reached their *clothes and were about to put our plan into action when Skimmy stood up with a ging in his hand, the other two followed suit. They had obviously been expecting someone to turn up and had planted their slingshots, together with ammunition, at the edge of the water.*

"Touch those clothes Collieflower and ya get a marble in the head." said Alan Campbell or Skimmy as we called him. Why we did I don't know but Skimmy was a nickname that stuck with him into his adult life. In turn he had referred to me as Collieflower: a nickname I detested, and his using it was almost a declaration of war. However, with the possibility of having three marbles fired at us from close range, now was not the time to discuss my dislike for that particular nickname.

"Wotcha talkin' about mate? Me an' Ginger was just gonna join ya for a dip."

"Pigs ying yang ya were! We seen ya hiding up on the bank." said the smaller of the two Convent boys.

To emphasize the point he stretched the rubbers of his ging a few extra inches. This was the straw that broke the camel's back. The piece of bike tube snapped with a resounding whack and as a result the broken end slapped the boy in the face just below the eye. He screamed in pain and for a moment no one, except Ginger and I, knew just what had happened. This distraction gave us the chance we needed to grab a handful of cloths and take off. Sadly, to our detriment, the other two recovered fairly quickly and as Ginger took a quick look over his shoulder a marble hit him just above his right ear. He dropped to the ground as if pole-axed with the right side of his face taking the full force of his fall. I stopped to see what had happened, thinking that he had just tripped over in his haste to escape, when another marble clouted me on the left elbow. By the time I had recovered enough to kneel beside my friend, his eyes had opened and he was attempting to sit up. "Wot the bloody hell happened?" he said spitting out dirt. He put his hand to his head and it came away sticky with blood.

"Looks like ya musta copped one in the nut mate," I said trying to show some sympathy while internally writhing with the pain in my elbow.

The three convent boys watched the proceedings from a safe distance, gings ready unless we decided to take immediate revenge. Skimmy was the first to speak. "Is he alright?" he stuttered. "I didn't mean to hit him in the head I was aiming at his bum."

Ginger and I looked at each other, knowing immediately that we would milk this for as long as we could. I stood up shaking my head;

"Well bloody good shot, Skimmy. He's bleeding pretty bad from the head. We'll have t' help him 'cause I reckon he'll need to go to the hospital for some stitches."

By this time the Convent trio had collected their clothes and put them on.

"We got our bikes an' could double ya." said the boy who had been smacked with the rubber. This sounded like a good idea and meant that they would have to double us to the hospital on the other side of town. The Convent boarders had to go that way as the school was just opposite the hospital. Skimmy on the other hand, lived near Ginger and said, "You blokes will have t' take 'em, 'cause I gotta go home."

So it was decided. However, the trip was not without incident for as we passed the Blue Bird Café, Ginger had a bit of a turn. I diagnosed concussion which had to be treated with milk. At this Ginger said, "The only way I can drink milk is when it is made into a shake with vanilla flavouring and double ice cream!"

The Convent boys conferred and while not particularly happy, grudgingly agreed to the treatment. This went down very well with Ginger but, in his delicate condition, he was only able to drink half.

"Finish 'er off mate." he said handing the glistening aluminum container to me. "I reckon you Convent blokes wouldn't want proddy germs would ya?" I said.

Not wanting to give them him time to decide if the risk of State school germs was worth a few mouthfuls of milkshake, I drank the remainder without taking a breath.

"That won't do me busted elbow any harm either," I said licking my lips.

A hundred or so yards from our destination the boys stopped, "D'ya reckon ya could walk from here?" they asked. "'Cause if the nuns see us doubling you two we'll be in strife."

Ginger and I exchanged glances and knew we had done as well out of the situation as we were going to.

"No worries, mate." I said; "We'll be able to make it from here."

It wasn't until after I had spoken that I realised that I had just called a couple of Convent school kids 'mate'. They were as surprised as Ginger and stammered their thanks. At this point I knew that the kids from behind the

Convent walls were not so different from us and were not a sub-species of child that we only ever met on the sports field.

"My name's John." I said sticking out my hand. "An' this is Ginger."

The taller of the two took my hand, "Oh we know who you two are," he said, "My name's Edwin and this is my brother Ray."

After handshakes all round it was agreed that the next time they were allowed out they would come around and we would all go for a swim together.

"They seemed OK sorta blokes, don't cha reckon?" said Ginger as we walked towards the hospital.

"Yep, not bad for cattle ticks." I replied trying to work out how we were going to explain our wounds to the matron as, by this time, my elbow was quite badly swollen.

As luck would have it the matron was not on duty and the sister was new and did not ask any embarrassing questions. Half an hour later Ginger had a bald patch and three stitches, while I sported a tight bandage, my arm in a sling, plus instructions that I had to return on Monday for an x-ray. As we trudged home from the hospital we discussed just what we would tell my parents, as we didn't want to get Skimmy or the Convent boys into any strife.

"The trouble is" said Ginger, "Your Mum's too bloody smart an' she'll sus something that's for sure."

"I reckon we just say we had a buster on a bike."

"Nar; we would have more skin off if we'd had a buster."

"Ya right. That idea was pretty dumb." I conceded, "Well, how about we had a friendly game of footy. Anything can happen when we do that."

"Yep, I reckon that'll do the trick."

Mum and Dad were sitting on the back steps with an afternoon cuppa when I arrived after saying goodbye to Ginger.

"Hello what have you been doing to yourself son?" asked Dad as soon as he saw the sling. "Aw just hurt my elbow playing footy. The sister said I gotta have an x-ray but I reckon it'll be OK."

This was not enough to satisfy Mum so after both parents had inspected the damaged elbow it was decided that an x-ray was probably not going to be necessary.

"The bruise is very neat and round," said my mother. "You must have fallen on something about the size of a marble."

As Ginger had said earlier Mum is wise to the ways of children, but to my relief in this instance she let the matter stop there. I am sure that the last comment had only been made so that I would know that she knew exactly what had happened.

The next day on school parade, as was the practice with new kids, Molly was introduced to everyone. However during the introduction, the headmaster told the assembly that Molly's father would be replacing Mr. Robbins on the Council. Now, this meant that all the children knew that Molly was the dunnyman's daughter. They would have found out anyway, but I thought it was a pretty mean way to be introduced.

The school was divided into two, with one teacher taking grades one to four and the headmaster taking five to eight. There were five of us in grade seven and seven in Ginger's grade six. Molly's inclusion in grade five moved its number to twelve, making it easily the largest in the school. Now, even before Molly's arrival, the head had threatened to put down some of the grade fives to grade four if they didn't pull up their socks. This threat was repeated when Molly was introduced to the class, but the real reason was probably because there were twenty-seven children in the top half of the school and only twenty-three in the lower.

At little lunch Molly sought me out to ask, "Am I really going to be put down to grade four? 'Cause that's not fair. I can do grade six sums an' can read better than me Dad."

"Ya don't have t' worry" I replied. "Old Woody won't do it."

She seemed a little relieved, and then inquired, "Why do you call the Headmaster' Woody'?"

"It's 'cause he's got a head like Woody Woodpecker."

"Well his hair does stick up at the back." she agreed, "But it's not nice to call people names and you should use his name - Mr. Golding."

Not wanting to be seen spending too much time with a grade five girl I ambled over to a group of boys who were arranging a football game for lunch time. As with all the impromptu team sports played during school, two captains had taken turns selecting the team of their choice. However, the teams rarely varied: the two grade eight boys were automatically the captains and they always picked mates and brothers of mates first.

Football was the only team sport that the girls weren't allowed to play and there were also strict codes with regard to how players played against anyone smaller than themselves. This meant that the boys in the lower half of the school *had no hesitation in playing against the bigger and stronger boys from the upper half. Anyone who did not obey the code was dealt with, sometime quite harshly, by the rest of the school, rarely needing the attention of the headmaster.*

As a boy I always felt that school could be tolerated because of the sport and social structure that it provided. I was an average student and don't think that I had suffered in any way from the nomadic life my family had led. Because my brothers and I had been the new boys at eight schools, we had learned to make friends quickly and establish ourselves with the minimum of fuss. This procedure usually took about a week and occasionally required a trip or two behind the boy's toilet, an area set aside in all State schools where the boys went to settle their differences.

Now, while some of these trips proved to be quite a painful experience they certainly accelerated the procedure that established where we fitted in to the order of things. When we moved to The Gully eighteen months previously, my older brother had gone away to high school, so this was the first time Edward and I had settled in on our own. We were lucky and things were settled with little pain and fuss. Now a year and a half later we were almost accepted as locals. We had never been at a school for this long before and for the first time in my life I felt a sense of belonging.

I look back now and ponder if this wonderful feeling of being part of the town had been a factor in my involvement, or lack of it with regard to Molly. I empathised with Molly and was more than willing to give her a hand to get established but I was totally unprepared and unskilled when it came to dealing with girls in this type of situation. With my own gender the area behind the boy's toilets was where these problems were sorted out.

As the weeks went by I knew she was not happy, but as my idea of communicating with girls was to dip their hair in an inkwell, I was not much help. Also perhaps I wasn't sure if I wanted to cash in some of my hard won local status on a little grade five girl. Oh! If I was around I did the right thing but perhaps I could have done more. The kids all called her 'DD' which stood for Dunnyman's Daughter. I told Mum that she was having a hard time and she spoke to Woody but he just said that the other children would soon tire of teasing her.

One Friday afternoon Ginger and I were on our way home from the creek when we saw Mr. Wodomo and Molly outside the caravan they rented in the fuel depot yard.

"G'day boys, been takin' a dip in the mud?" he said smiling.

"G'day Mr. Wodomo." we both replied.

"G'day Molly." I went on, "Were ya crook t'day? 'Cause I didn't see ya at school."

At that moment the door of the caravan opened and a lady we had never seen before stuck her head out.

"Tex, give me a hand in here will ya. I don't know how you and the brat can live in this dump."

"Vivian," he said "This is Blondie and Ginger. They're Molly's mates an' they look out for her at school. Boys this is Vivian."

"Pleased t' meet cha Mrs. Wodomo," we both replied.

"I'm not Mrs. bloody Wodomo." she exploded. "That bitch done a runner. I'm just a friend he met in the Isa. Molly why don't ya go for a walk with the boys so me and ya Dad can ... er, do something."

Molly immediately started towards the gate; we said our goodbyes and followed her.

"Don't cha like ya Dad's friend?" asked Ginger.

Molly stopped and looked back at the caravan. "Oh she's alright, but she likes to jump all the time I don't like it when they do that."

Now while Ginger and I might have thought we knew what she meant we couldn't believe that she would just come out and say it.

"Er wot do ya mean she likes to jump?" I ventured.

"I don't know." came the reply. "But she often tells me to clear off for a while 'cause she wants to jump me Dad. She can't tell me to clear off from where I live can she? Anyway I don't have to worry, she'll be off soon, same as the others. Same as me Mum did too."

"It must be funny not having a Mum," said Ginger. "I don't mean the laughing sort of funny, but you know different sorta."

"It's alright when Dad hasn't got a girlfriend. Me Dad and I are good mates, but when there is three of us we can't seem to be happy. I reckon it's got to do with the jumping."

We agreed that was the probable reason for whatever it was Molly was talking about. This was the fifties and both of us were having a lot of trouble understanding the situation that Molly lived in. Rightly or wrongly it was always the man who left the woman with the children and not the other way around as in this case. Also, for that man to have girlfriends who liked 'jumping' was just too much to comprehend. For us it was exciting and titillating but for poor Molly it must have been very confusing and painful. As if being the dunnyman's daughter wasn't bad enough, we knew her tormentors at school would have a field day with this little bit of gossip.

"I don't reckon ya should tell anyone that Vivian isn't ya Mum." I muttered as off-handedly as I possibly could.

Ginger gave a very positive grunt of agreement while picking at the scab that was forming nicely over the cut on his head.

"I wouldn't tell a soul." said Molly firmly, "But that Vivian doesn't want anyone to think that she is saddled with a kid, so she makes sure that everyone knows that I am not hers."

Our journey home on that particular afternoon took us right passed old man Wallis's garage. The place itself was nothing in particular and very typical of country workshops but this one was interesting by virtue of the fact that Mr. Wallis was a pilot of some renown and quite often would be working on one of his machines. We were in luck. An old Cessna was parked on the side of the road next to the workshop and Mr. Wallis and his mechanic were obviously celebrating a job well done with a cold beer.

"G'day Mr. Wallis." I called, "Been doin' a bitta work on 'er?"

Mr. Wallis acknowledged Ginger and I with a nod, "Yep. Just put new pistons in the old girl, ya can take a look inside if ya wanna, but don't touch nothing."

"Aw beauty thanks Mr. Wallis." we replied.

The inside of the machine appeared to be a mass of gauges, levers and buttons.

"Wow!" said Ginger, "I reckon you'd have to be pretty smart t' know what t' push and what t' pull."

The old pilot overheard this comment and wandered over to us. It was immediately obvious that the bottle of beer in his hand was by no means his first for the afternoon. He tussled Ginger's hair.

"So ya reckon I'm smart do ya young fella? It's not a lot different to drivin' a car; just a few more things t' remember."

I looked at him as he spoke and I saw a face that had seen far too many western Queensland summers plus a world war. I could see and hear more than just a hint of pride in what this man had achieved in this machine and others like it.

"Look" he said, "As soon as me an' Danny finish our beers we are gonna take 'er up for a run. If ya wanna come up ya welcome." He looked hard at me before finishing, "But you Blondie, you gotta ask Arthur first 'cause I know he would want ya to."

"Aw I don't think he would mind Mr. Wallis. I know he reckons you are a great pilot especially after that night ya landed with just a mob of car lights t' show ya where the strip was, an' ya wouldn't be long would ya?"

"Pull the other leg Blondie, your old man would be cranky as a cut snake but that wouldn't be half as bad as ya Mum. No, you bugger off an' if ya get the OK come on back. We still got a couple to knock off before we leave."

In the five-minute walk from the Wallis garage to my house Ginger and I covered at least a dozen different tacks I could try on one of my parents in an effort to get permission for the flight.

"How come he didn't tell you to get permission?" I asked my mate.

"I reckon its 'cause he's one of me old mans drinkin' mates an' he knows me old man couldn't give a damn what I done." Ginger replied, in a voice that indicated he might have been pleased if parental permission had been required.

As soon as I saw that both my parents were at home I knew my chance of getting permission would be almost zero.

"Gee wiz," I exclaimed "I'll never be able to talk both of 'em round. Just my luck! A chance to fly with someone who got shot down in the war, an' I'll bet I won't be allowed." I was quite right, both my parents were adamant that I would not be given permission under any circumstances.

"But it's quite safe!" I pleaded "Him and Mr. Holmund have just put a new piston in the 'plane an' even you reckon he's a top pilot, Dad."

"If he and Danny Holmund have been working on the plane together they will also have been on the grog." my mother interjected. My face must have been a real give-away as she carried on, "I'm right aren't I? They are on the grog?"

At this point I heard the sound of the 'plane engine revving and I knew from previous experience that this was a signal to all motorists that the only bitumen road in the town was about to be used as a runway. This road ran from the centre of town past the Wallis garage, past our house, which was in the last street going north. Once past our street the bitumen road slowly curved to the left, crossed a small gully and in a Y junction met a road that came from the other end of town. Dad reckoned the only reason that it had been surfaced was so that the cemetery could be reached during the wet season.

The distance from the Wallis garage to where the road started to curve was probably less than three hundred yards, barely enough time for the Cessna to be airborne. Even though I was disappointed not to be on board, Ginger and I scrambled onto the roof to get a bird's eye view of the takeoff. As the 'plane whizzed past our house we could clearly see its three occupants, two of them toasting us with a bottle of beer. We waved in reply and watched as the wheels lost contact with the earth and the tiny aircraft struggled to make height. I don't know what happened next but when it was at about thirty feet off the ground the' plane gracefully rolled over onto its back. We both went "Wow!" thinking the manoeuvre had been done to impress us but this quickly turned to horror as we watched the left wing slice the top off a large Christ-thorn tree on the edge of the gully before the plane crashed upside down in the middle of the other road that made up the Y junction. With a sound similar to chalk on a blackboard the craft slid across the gravel surface, cart wheeling to put it right side up as the engine ploughed into the table drain on the far side of the road.

Ginger and I stared in disbelief as a huge cloud of dust engulfed the entire scene. This trance-like state was broken by my father yelling as he and Mum ran for the car, first-aid kit in hand.

"John, is it on fire?"

"Don't think so." I replied.

"I have rung the ambulance but will you go over to the Council quarters, find Mr. Williams and ask him to bring the water truck out just in case," he called as the car sped off to the crash site.

A final look brought me to a sudden stop, as, from the base of the Christ-thorn tree, I saw someone stand up and slowly stumble towards the 'plane.

"Bloody hell!" said Ginger "Do ya reckon someone was up the tree when she hit it?"

"Na, ya know no one can climb that thorny damn tree, maybe he was just sittin' there."

"Probably that's more likely, but I'll bet he needs a change of strides."

As we made our way down from the roof and then over to the Council yards I wondered what type of injuries my parents would be called on to treat and who the mystery person under the tree was. I knew the injured would be in good hands as both my parents were qualified voluntary ambulance bearers and had attended a number of bad road accidents. We arrived at the Council complex to find Mr. Williams washing the front verandah of his flat. He agreed to immediately grab the water truck and head out to the accident site.

"D'ya reckon me an' Ginger could come with ya?" I asked hopefully.

"From what you said I don't reckon that would be a good idea young Blondie," he replied over his shoulder, already on his way to the Council yards.

"Come on let's leg it out there and have a look for ourselves." said Ginger as the Council water truck roared past us.

"My oath!" I replied "We seen it crash so it's only right that we get to have a look at the wreck."

As we picked our way through the clumps of dry grass that grew sparsely on the town common we could see that quite a number of cars were at the site already. As we neared the tree that had been hit we saw the ambulance leave, lights flashing, closely followed by my parents' car. For me this was a good sign as the only other person that would tell Ginger and I to leave would be the police sergeant and I was confident we could avoid him.

"Wow!" exclaimed my redheaded mate. "Bloody fixed up the ol' Christ-thorn tree don't cha reckon?"

"My oath! We won't get any more chinky apples from that tree that's for sure."

By now we were walking through the mass of cars that surrounded the crashed aircraft and the scene was one of organised chaos with the Sarge trying to get people to move their cars so that Mr. Williams could get in with the water truck. Finally, he climbed onto the back of the police Ute and yelled at the top of his voice. "Any bloody vehicle that is not moved ..." here he stopped and looked directly at Ginger and I. "Blondie, you run a hundred yards up the road that way and Ginger, you go a hundred yards towards town.

Now, as I was saying any bloody vehicle closer to the 'plane than Blondie and Ginger will be put off the road for a month. Now move!"

I walked to what was actually a pretty short hundred yards before I could even get a decent look at the wreck but as the cars started to clear, the shock of seeing the mangled remains of something that I had seriously contemplated disobeying my parents and going for a ride in, hit me like a sledgehammer. The gouge where it had hit the road was two foot wide and probably just as deep. This went across the road and there was a huge hole where it had ploughed into the table drain. The 'plane itself was a complete wreck with the engine twisted at right angles to the remains of the fuselage and almost into the area where the passenger next to the pilot would have been sitting. One wing was almost detached, while the tail section bore no resemblance to its original shape. The entire area was covered in oil and fuel and it wasn't difficult to see why the Sarge had wanted the area cleared. One vehicle, however, had not moved as instructed and it was only when the others had gone that I saw my father. He was giving medical attention to a man sitting on the vehicle's tailgate; while he had a bandage around his head he was sitting up without help and seemed to be talking to Dad. When the last of the vehicles had moved, with most of them having seen enough and headed home, I decided it was time for me to have a closer look.

As I approached my father I recognised his patient as Mr. Holmund, the mechanic from Wallis's garage. He looked up and then said to Dad, "Bloody good thing ya didn't let young Blondie come with us, Arthur."

Dad acknowledged my arrival then said, "Keep still Danny, you have still got one Christ-thorn in the side of your neck."

A second later with the relish of someone who had just found gold he pulled a two inch thorn from the man's neck, holding it up in triumph for all to see.

"Aw, bloody beauty, Arthur that was hurtin' like a mongrel." He turned away from us and spat a mouthful of blood before continuing. "By the look of where the engine finished up I reckon I'm the luckiest bloke west of Brisbane."

"I'll go along with that." said Dad "However you have got to let the hospital take a look at that head cut and I am sure you will need something for the pain as well as that cut in your mouth."

He shook his head, "No bloody hospitals for me, you done a good job Arthur an' I know just the medicine that'll fix me up."

At this point my father stepped back and, from the set of his jaw and slight narrowing of his eyes I knew Mr. Holmund was going to be advised in, perhaps stronger terms.

"You listen to me Danny." said Dad through clenched teeth. "Don't be any bigger idiot then you have been already. The actions of you and your drunken mates could have cost lives today. How you all lived through that mess behind me I don't know, but this I do know, I am not going to spend any more time patching you up if all you are going to do is get stuck into the grog again."

After letting that outburst sink in he continued in the same tone, "Appreciate your second shot at life. People a lot better than you never get that opportunity."

In the almost fifty years that I knew my father I never heard him speak like that again and by his reply Mr. Holmund was as surprised as myself.

"Er! So ya reckon I should let the matron take a look at me?"

"The flying Doctor is on his way and should be here in about an hour so let's get you into hospital and ready for him to have a good look at you."

"I reckon ya right Arthur, an' I'm.,... er sorry for being an idiot." he said with a painful grin.

Dad accepted the man's apology without a word; instead he went over to the owner of the vehicle they were using and he made arrangements for his patient to be taken to the hospital, stressing that it was not to be via the pub. By now Mr. Williams had flooded the area immediately around the plane and the Sarge had put blobs of paint to show where pieces of the craft had been picked up, muttering all the time about what the clowns from the DCA expected him to do.

Ginger and I at last went right over to the plane and it wasn't until then that I realised the significance of the thorns Dad had removed from Mr. Holmund. No one sitting where he was when they went passed our house could have lived through the crash as the seat and dash on that side was crushed when the engine had been torn round to that side.

"Ya know what happened don't ya mate?" I said to Ginger who had not seen the thorns taken out and not waiting for him to reply I continued "Mr. Homund musta been the bloke we seen coming from under the tree. I reckon he fell out when the plane hit the tree."

At this time the Sarge and Dad came over to us,

"Your Dad tells me you pair of tearaways were actually watching the take off an' saw what happened." he said to me.

"Yes sir, we seen it happen." we both replied.

Keen to test my theory, I continued "I reckon Mr. Holmund fell out when she hit the tree upside down as me and Ginger seen someone come from under the tree."

"I think ya right Blondie." said the Sarge. "But I want you boys to go home *and write down exactly what you saw. Don't do it together and keep it about a page. Don't put down what you think happened, just what you saw. OK?"*

Being the only witnesses to the crash gave Ginger and I local status usually reserved for people like the bank manager. People who never normally gave us the time of the day, went out of their way to say "Hello" and everyone wanted to hear first-hand what had happened.

The upshot of the inquiry was that the 'plane had experienced a severe crosswind while taking off; this had flipped it onto its back. When it hit the tree the passenger's door had flown open and Mr. Holman had fallen from the craft. The other two occupants had suffered injuries ranging from a broken leg to facial cuts when the 'plane had crashed onto the road.

It was obvious that those two had their seat belts on at the time of impact, a factor that certainly contributed to their surviving the crash. Whereas it was found that if Mr. Holmund had put his on he would not have fallen out and would most certainly have died. As it was in those days, not a lot was said about the physical state of the pilot prior to him taking off, and I am sure the whole thing was just put down as 'an accident.'

****

Sadly, the completion of the enquiry also heralded the end of our elevated position in the community but it was great while it lasted. Maybe during this period I got a bit big headed and it wasn't until I thudded back to reality that I noticed that Molly was having a particularly rough time because everyone now knew about the living arrangements at the caravan. This situation was not helped when one-day "Woody" asked her to bring her mother in, as he wanted to talk to her. Now, I am sure that he knew that the woman living with Tex was not related in any way, but for some reason he just had it in for Molly.

"My Mother doesn't live here." stammered the embarrassed girl.

"Don't lie to me girl!" he thundered, "I have seen her sitting outside the van you live in."

"That woman is not me Mum" came the whispered answer.

"You mean that woman living in the van with your father and you is not your mother? That's disgusting and if I had my way you would be taken away and put into a home."

I expected Molly to burst into tears but she just sat there with her jaw clenched and her eyes fixed on the Headmaster. After a stand-off lasting about a minute it was the Head that made the first move.

"*Don't you stare at me you impertinent child. Go out and stand on the verandah.*"

The class laughed as she left the room and once again I felt ashamed that I had not made a stand on the girl's behalf. I don't know what I could have done but I am sure any sign of support would have helped. That afternoon the boys had football practice, an event that was looked forward to each week as Mr. Lord who worked in the bank, would come to coach us. The Headmaster, Mr. Golding, would help him but, for that short time, we were not directly under his charge. I don't know why, but it always felt good to see him taking directions from someone else. I always felt that Mr. Lord would have preferred it if he had been left on his own, but that would have meant that Mr. Golding would not be totally in charge and I don't reckon he would have gone for that.

It was my turn to put the gear away and turning the corner to the gear room, I once again nearly fell over Molly.

"*What the hell ya still doin' here?*" I asked.

It was obvious that she had been crying however her voice still had that defiance in it.

"*Nobody told me I could leave, so I just stayed.*"

"*Hell!*" I exclaimed, "*It must be about past five o'clock. Woody don't keep anyone in 'till this time. I reckon he musta forgot ya.*" By the time I returned to the team Mr. Golding had left but as the headmaster's house was always in the schoolyard, it was no problem to go and tell him about Molly.

The headmaster's wife, a woman who never smiled or seemed happy, answered my knock on the door. She was a small bird-like person who spoke to the children in her husband's charge only when it was absolutory necessary.

"*What is it you want?*" she asked, peering around the edge of the only slightly open door.

"*Excuse me Mrs. Golding, but I think that Mr. Golding musta forgot about Molly 'cause she's still on the verandah an' I reckon her old man might be wondering where she is.*"

At this point the head's voice boomed from inside as he had obviously been listening. "*Tiley! If that stupid friend of yours hasn't even got the brains to go home it certainly is not my fault. Now you go back and tell that silly girl her detention was over almost two hours ago.*"

As we walked home a little later I asked, "*Wot ya gonna tell ya old man?*

I reckon ya should tell him the whole story an' maybe he'll go in an' sort Woody out."

Molly shook her head. "That won't fix nothing 'cause my old man is just the dunnyman and people don't talk to the dunnyman."

In my heart I knew a lot of what she said was true, but felt that her father should be told of the way she was being treated at school.

"Aw that's not true, I know some people think like that, but not many; the same thing with Ginger 'cause his Mum and Dad drink a lot an' fight sometimes."

"That's different, when Dad an' I go shopping on Saturday some people might nod at us but very few say g'day and nobody will stop to have a yarn. I know me Dad doesn't like being a dunnyman but he does it so I can go to school. He is different to a lot of Dads; he doesn't drink beer and is a good bloke an' people should be nice to good blokes. Your Mum an' Dad always are."

Here the flow of words stopped and the tears started. I was stumped and didn't have a clue what to do.

"Er! Do ya wanna come over tomorra? Ginger an' I will probably be doing something an' I reckon you could come or I got some comics that ya can read."

The tears slowed to a trickle, "C...c...can't" she sobbed, "I gotta go shopping with me Dad."

"Boy, that's pretty mean makin' ya go shopping, I gotta do a lot of things like chopping wood, washing up an' makin' me bed but even my parents don't make me do the shoppin'."

To my absolute surprise Molly looked at me and said, "I love shopping with Dad, an' he reckons I am good at picking the fruit and veggies. We always go to the Blue Bird Café when we are finished at the grocers. Dad has a coffee an' I have a chocolate milkshake."

After we had parted I contemplated whether or not to tell my mother about what had happened. Knowing that she would talk to Woody and he would then take it out on me I decided that in this instance the Wodomos should look after this themselves.

Molly hadn't been to school for a few days so Ginger and I stopped at her caravan one afternoon on our way home from school.

"G'day Mr. Wodomo. How are ya?" I asked when he answered our knock.

"Pretty good thanks boys, what can I do for ya?"

147

"Aw, we figured that Molly musta been crook, so just dropped in to see if she was OK."

His eyes told me that something was not right. "Boys I don't know what the problem is, but she got home real late last Friday. Wouldn't tell me where she had been, an' this week flat refuses to go to school. I was comin' in t' to have a yarn, John, to see if you knew what was up."

At this moment Molly appeared behind her father. "They don't know nothing" she said holding my attention with a fierce stare.

"Molly love" said Mr. Wodomo turning to his daughter. "I know something is not right an' if you won't tell me then I reckon young John here just might."

They both turned their attention back to Ginger and waited for some kind of response.

"Er …! I didn't go to footy training on Friday so I dunno what happened." said Ginger with a gulp.

Immediately Mr. Wodomo picked up on what my friend had said, "I knew that something happened on Friday. Well I don't need anyone to tell me 'cause I am off to see the teacher and ask him. I've had enough of this rubbish."

At that he grabbed his hat from where it was hanging outside, rammed it on his head and strode off towards the school. Molly started to cry, went inside and slammed the door shaking the entire caravan.

The next day Molly was back at school but there was a distinct coolness between her and the Headmaster. At lunchtime I asked, "Did ya old man go and see Woody?"

"Yes he did." come the reply, "An' Mr. Golding told Dad I wasn't smart enough to be in grade five and he was putting me down."

"Aw that's crazy." I retorted "There are lots of kids that should go down before you."

"I know that, but Dad doesn't understand and he just believes what the teachers tell him."

Later that day it was announced that Molly and one of the Lock brothers were being put down into grade four. The entire room was surprised at Molly being put down and I was determined to speak up; however when the Head answered my hand in the air with a curt "And what would you want Tiley?" I lost my nerve and asked.

"Er … will Lockie still be able to play footie Sir?"

As if he knew that was not what I had intended to say, the Head ignored

*my question and continued to watch the two children gather their books ready
for the move to the other room. During the lunch hour I found Molly sitting
in a corner under the school.*

"Wotcha doin'?" I asked, knowing full well what the answer would be.

"Nothin', just thinkin'."

"I reckon we'll be startin' a game of rounders soon, wanna be on my side?"

*Rounders was played with a stick and a rubber ball, usually a worn out
one from the tennis club. It is a little like baseball except a ball caught on the
full meant that the whole team was out. If it was caught after one bounce only
the batter was out. Anyone running the bases was tagged out with the ball if
not on the base. Unlike baseball, the ball could be thrown at the runner to tag
or brand them out. This could be painful at times so the unwritten rules stated
that you were not to throw hard at any of the girls playing, especially those
from the lower half of the school. Now Molly was a good rounders player by
any standard and especially good for a girl. She loved to play and was proud
of her ability to hit the ball hard and dodge when an attempt was made to
'brand' her out.*

*"Come on Molly give it a clout." encouraged Ginger as she took the bat
and walked to the home base.*

*The pitcher took a couple of paces forward as was the custom when
throwing the ball to the smaller kids from grades one to four. "Wotcha doin'?"
she demanded.*

*In a sing song voice the reply came, "Got to be careful not to throw too hard
for the school babies, come on now try to hit the ball Dee Dee."*

*Angered by the taunts, Molly gripped the bat so that the whites of her
knuckles showed and when the ball was lobbed to her she swung so hard she
missed it by a country mile.*

*The pitcher mocked "Now, now Dee Dee just try to hit the ball, then you
run as fast as your little legs will carry you to first base."*

*"Come on!," I called from third. "Give her a decent throw an' I reckon
she'll belt ya to the fence."*

"Shut ya gob Tiley. I'll throw what I like to the dunnyman's daughter."

*The second throw was much the same as the first and again anger caused
Molly to swing and miss.*

The fielding team taunted her with a loud "Wow!"

149

Molly shuffled her feet and from third I could see she was struggling to hold back tears.

"Oh now the bubbie is going to cry." said Helen Hardy the grade six girl who was pitching. "Maybe we should get her Mummy to wipe her snotty nose an' teach her to bat. But can't do that 'cause she buggered off: couldn't stand the smell of her old man I reckon."

A few kids laughed and Helen took a little bow, in doing so turned her back to Molly and therefore did not see the attack coming. Years of pent up frustration and anger came to the surface at that moment as the broom handle bat landed with a crack across Helens shoulders. She went down like a pole-axed bullock but immediately rolled away so as to avoid any further attack. However by now Ginger and I had hold of Molly who was shaking and crying uncontrollably.

"You must not say things about me Dad!" she screamed.

"You're bloody mad ya little bitch" said the pitcher holding out her hand to show that her elbow was bleeding.

The crowd attracted the attention of the headmaster who by now was striding across the playground towards us and I knew that Molly was going to be in big strife.

"Helen I'll give ya a bunch of comics if ya tell Woody it was an accident," I pleaded.

"Go jump in the lake Collie dog, I'm gonna tell him to get the police an' I reckon the Dunnyman's daughter'll go t' jail."

Even though Helen was not badly hurt the headmaster sent her to the hospital to be checked out and have her elbow dressed. Later that afternoon her parents arrived at the school with the police sergeant. Molly had not spoken since the incident so I decided to put her side to the Headmaster.

"Please Sir!" I blurted out, "It wasn't all Molly's fault, Helen was teasing her."

"So a little teasing gives her the right to smash someone with a baseball bat does it Tiley?"

"Well er not really Sir but…"

"No buts boy!" he interjected "This was an assault and I am pleased that Mr. and Mrs. Hardy have decided to involve the police in the matter."

I found out later that Molly did not say one word when asked why she had hit Helen, which meant that the Sarge and her parents only heard one side of the story. That afternoon after Dad got home from work Mr. Wodomo and Molly turned up at our house, "Arthur could I have a word with young John?" he asked my father.

"No worries Tex, John has already told me all about what happened."

"That's the problem. Molly just handed me a letter from the Headmaster. My lady friend read it an' says that Molly is suspended from school for two weeks for fighting. Molly won't talk so I am buggered if I know what to do."

Dad took the letter from his outstretched hand read it quickly before handing it on to Mum who read it more carefully; she returned it to Mr. Wodomo saying,

"I have heard Molly's side of the story from John and I think you should as well. Sit down and I'll make a brew. Molly, you come and give me a hand while your dad talks to John."

As I told exactly what happened, the man's dark brown eyes never left mine. When I had finished he asked, "Do you think what Molly did was wrong?"

"Er ... not really 'cause Helen said some pretty awful stuff."

"But not enough to deserve a wack with a stick eh?" he said with a hint of anger in his voice.

"Maybe, but Helen is bigger than Molly an' she was just standing up for her family. The kids give her a bit of stick ya know an' I reckon she'd just had enough."

The poor man was clearly confused over what was expected of him and was relieved when Mum and Molly arrived with the tea and cake. "John" she said, "You and Molly take your cordial and cake out onto the verandah, I am sure you have some comics that she can read."

I didn't want to as I knew some interesting conversation would ensue, however, I knew where to sit, out of sight and still be able to hear reasonably well.

"I dunno what t' do missus. Molly is a good kid and has never done anything like this before." My mother replied, "Don't blame Molly too much Tex. Kids can be cruel, you know, and from what John says she normally just takes it."

Here my dad spoke, "I don't think you should do anything more about the affair. I think the Headmaster handled the entire thing badly. Molly should never have had to face up to the Sergeant and the other girl's parents by herself."

"I agree," said Mum "Molly is clearly deeply upset by what she did and I don't think she looks well. Just keep her home for the two weeks and things will have settled down by the time she returns."

"Do you think that the police will want to see Molly again?"

"No Tex," said Dad "I certainly wouldn't worry about that. I am sure that the Sarge was only involved because of Mrs. Hardy. I know Jack Hardy pretty well and he is aware that their young Helen can be spiteful at times."

After they had gone and I was cleaning up the dishes, Mum remarked, "You know, that girl never said a word all the time she was here."

Dad replied, "She never has a lot to say, but I agree she doesn't look well. I'll talk to Tex about letting matron have a look at her, but he doesn't go much on that sort of thing."

I didn't see Molly for the two weeks that she was suspended because Ginger and I had been given an old bike that we were 'doing up'. The wet season had started and the town had been flood-bound for the last few days. I loved this time of the year; the creek was running and the whole countryside seemed to come to life. What, a week before, had looked old, rusty and worn out, now glistened and seemed to take on a new lease of life. This was the best rain we had had for two years and, as if by magic, budgies by the thousands started to appear in the trees along the creek. Overnight the dead-looking clumps of grass took on a green hue and huge flocks of these birds would land on a patch that looked the greenest and would literally strip it of colour.

Ginger and I were on our way to look for nests and perhaps snare a couple of budgies and try to sell them. On the way we saw Molly sitting outside of the caravan, "G'day Molly how ya been goin'?"

She acknowledged our greeting by a little wave but didn't speak to us. At this moment her stepmother, as we called her for want of a better name, came out.

"It's no good talkin' to the dummy, boys. She don't say nothin', just nods like a donkey."

I didn't believe that Molly wouldn't talk to us and asked, "Wanna come to the creek with me and Ginger? We reckon we might be able to get a couple of budgies an' you can keep one if we do."

"Yep!" said Ginger. "We got a special tree that we'll show ya. It's always got a nest in it an' you can probably get a real young one that ya can teach to talk."

We could see from her face that she wanted to go but instead of saying so *she just got up, put her hat on and started walking in the direction of the creek. Ginger and I shrugged our shoulders and ambled after her, "Hold up Molly, it's not a race ya know!" I called.*

We soon caught her up and while we wondered why she was not talking didn't push her to join in the conversation. The rain-soaked black soil built up on our feet and from time to time had to be kicked off. Usually when you did this the mud was aimed at another member of the group but on this occasion Ginger and I contested to see who could kick the mud further. Molly didn't join in but did relax a little and even smiled when a piece of mud Ginger kicked off flew straight up and landed on her back.

The creek was still running a banker and was too inviting to pass up. "Comin' in?" I asked Molly.

She shook her head and sat down indicating that she would watch Ginger and me. Normally we would have gone in the nude but mixed company demanded we wear our shorts. They would dry in no time so we weren't worried.

"Come on Molly!" I asked again "Ya can wear ya clothes in an' they'll dry before we go home." I then remembered that Ginger had mentioned our special budgie tree.

"If ya want to come to the budgie tree ya gotta swim across or walk up to the bridge."

She immediately started walking in the direction of the railway bridge. It was only about five or six hundred yards upstream from where we were swimming so we knew it wouldn't take her too long to get back to us. In fact by the time we had cooled off and had swum to the other side she was waiting for us.

The budgie tree was an ancient gum about half a mile from the creek; it had borne the brunt of many a storm and had the scars to prove it. The hollows left in the many broken branches were a haven to the thousands of budgies looking for a place to nest. What made this tree so special was that, for a gum, the main trunk divided close to the ground. One section went almost straight up with the other going off at about forty-five degrees and forking again after about six feet. This whole set-up made it an ideal tree for climbing and it was relatively easy for us to get up into a section of the tree where the budgies nested. It was also easy to sit in the second fork and watch the birds going to and from their nests. *This way you could get a good look at the babies and decide if they were old enough to live if you removed them from the nest.*

"*Wotcha like at climbin' trees, Molly?*" *Ginger asked.*

She still didn't talk but indicated that she was willing to get up into the branches and have a good look at the birds.

"*I reckon I'll go up first an' take a look first.*" *continued Ginger.*

"*Good idea mate. Have a decco for any joe blakes. Remember that one we saw the last time we were here.*"

"*Sure do, I nearly got me head stuck in the fork as I slipped between it to get out of his way.*"

"*Ya know.*" *I said* "*If ya did slip through that fork and get ya head stuck you'd be in a bit of strife.*"

"*Well it won't happen t' me again 'cause it just about ripped me bloody ears off last time.*" *Ginger called over his shoulder as he started to climb. The fork in question was about fifteen feet from the ground and our usual way of getting down from the tree was to have a hand on each branch, slip through the fork, hang and then drop to the ground. My mate quickly reached the fork and continued on to have a look at some nests further up.*

"*A couple have hatched up here but none of those in the nests around the lower branches,*" *he called down to us.*

Molly looked at me as if asking permission to climb. "*It's up to you.*" *I said* "*But I reckon in a week or so there will be lots to look at, an' ya can grab one for a pet if ya wanna.*"

She didn't climb the tree that day and to our surprise as we left she said, "*Dad doesn't like birds in cages, he reckons it's cruel. But I would like t' see them in their nests an' maybe touch one a little.*"

We were quite taken aback by this sudden return to voice and I replied, "*I reckon that'll be jake by next weekend. Wotcha reckon Ginger?*"

He nodded, "*Piece of cake, see ya at school t'morra.*"

The heavens really opened up in the first part of the following week. This meant that during the breaks at school all the kids crammed underneath the building and tried to amuse themselves. I noticed that during these periods Molly always sat alone and read. She always had the appearance of a drowned rat: this being the result of her walking to school in the morning without a raincoat. I spoke to her a couple of times during that week and on one occasion asked, "*Ya gonna come to the budgie tree on the weekend?*"

She looked at me in a strange way and said, "Angela Green reckons you're me friend 'cause ya Mum makes ya."

Again I was totally unprepared or equipped to deal with the reason behind her making a statement like that and before walking away I muttered, "Wot would that dumb Sheila know about anything?"

Friday saw the weather clear enough for us at least to get out from under the school in order to organise a game of rounders. When the teams had been picked, Ginger remarked to me, "Molly must be reading under the school, d' ya want me t' go over and get her?"

"Naw!" I replied, "I don't reckon she'll want t' play."

"She sick or something? She looked crook when I seen her the other day."

"Dunno mate, she hasn't been happy for a while, an' me Mum said ya can get crook if ya unhappy."

"Get out! Ya pullin' me leg!"

"No! Fair dinkum, Ginger, that's what Mum said."

We dropped the subject of Molly, as the game got under way but later when class had resumed I had reason to go to the lower grades section of the school, and during this visit noticed that Molly was not there. Walking home that afternoon with Ginger and my brother, Edward, we passed Mr.Wodomo's lady friend.

"Good afternoon boys." she greeted us. "Molly not walking home with you today?"

I quickly answered, "We had t' go to footy training and musta missed her."

"No worries, she is big enough and ugly enough to look after herself" she replied and continued on her way.

Once out of earshot Ginger said, "Well I'll be a monkey's uncle, what d' ya know! Molly musta played the wag t'day."

Here Edward piped up and said, "She wasn't at school yesterday either, an' other days. She got into lots of trouble 'cause she wouldn't talk to Miss Berry."

Wagging it from school was fairly rare as there were few places a kid could hide where they would not be seen by parents, friends or the local sergeant. Also, it was a small town and teachers met regularly with parents so the risk of being found out was very high.

"Wow!" said Ginger, "She must have a lot of guts t' play the wag for two days."

"Yes." I agreed, "Not even you would try that. Where d' ya reckon she went during the day?"

"Musta gone to the creek. 'Cause of the rain the Sarge wouldn't drive down there."

We didn't think too much about Molly's absence until later that evening when a knock at our front door interrupted dinner.

"Are ya there Arthur?" Mr. Wodomo called.

"Come through, Tex" replied Dad.

He came through to the kitchen where we were eating.

"Sorry to interrupt ya dinner, but I was wondering if John saw Molly after school today?"

Dad looked at me for an answer, "Er, no I never seen her."

"Edward?" asked my Mother, "Did you see Molly after school today?"

My young brother was obviously confused. He realised the seriousness of the situation but didn't want to dob Molly in for playing the wag. My Mother picked up straight away that something was not just right, "She was at school today wasn't she?"

Edward looked at me for support so I answered, "I don't think that she was."

Mr. Wodomo was clearly shocked by this information. "But if she didn't go to school" he spluttered, "Where did she go?"

"Ginger reckons she musta gone to the creek 'cause it's easy t' hide down there."

Here my Dad took over, "It's already dark outside, but we had better get a mob together and go and look for her. I'll get some of the boys from the Council quarters. Isobel you go and tell the Sarge and pick up whoever you can. We will all meet at the Turkey Nest in half an hour. If she is home by then there will be no damage done, if not, we will at least be able to search some areas tonight."

The night was a long wet one for the searchers and at breakfast the next morning I asked Mum, "Did they find Molly yet?"

"No," she replied "The damn rain made things very difficult, but they did find her school bag near the bridge. Old George the black tracker is coming in from Red Gum station but I don't know if he will be able to pick up her tracks with all this rain."

About this time my Dad and the Sergeant arrived. After Mum had given them a mug of steaming hot tea the Sergeant asked me, "If Molly was hiding where d' ya reckon she would go, John?" I thought for a while and it wasn't until I remembered Mum saying that her bag had been found near the bridge that I thought of the budgie tree.

"Me an' Ginger have got a special tree where a lot of budgies nest. We took Molly there once and she really liked it 'cause she could watch the birds up close."

"Good on ya mate," he replied, "Where is this special tree?"

"I can take ya there in a flash, it's pretty easy t' find."

Dad and the policeman exchanged glances before Dad said, "Just explain where it is son, we'll be able to find it easy enough."

I gave them details of where the tree was and the best way for them to get there. They must have thought it was a pretty good place to look as they left almost immediately. Ginger and I were sitting on the verandah reading comics when Dad arrived home about two hours later. The night's searching was starting to show. His eyes were bloodshot and he walked slowly as if measuring each step. He acknowledged us with a grunt, which was unusual as Dad always prided himself in speaking clearly. We followed him into the kitchen where he plonked himself onto a chair.

"Have you found her?" Mum asked.

Dad looked up and slowly nodded. Mum immediately turned to us kids saying,

"You lot go off for a while and swap some comics. Dad needs a hot shower and a cup of tea."

We went over to Skimmy's, swapped a few but all we talked about was the search for Molly. Skimmy's Dad was out with the search and arrived home as we were leaving. Like my Dad he was soaking wet and almost as grim-faced.

"I just come from your place, John, an' ya Dad said t' send ya straight home."

"OK Mr. Campbell. We're off. See ya."

The police utility was outside when we arrived home and while we knew something was not right we were still treating the situation like an adventure. We were therefore surprised to find not only my parents and the Sarge in the sitting room but also Matron from the hospital and Mr. Kenny the ambulance man. My father was the first to speak,

"Hold up boys, we have something to tell you."

The three of us sat on the floor with our backs against the wall and waited *for the news of our friend. I expected Dad to continue talking, however, the matron picked up her chair and sat squarely in front of us.*

"I am sorry to have to tell you this, boys, but when they found Molly this morning I am afraid she was dead."

I was confused as up until now death had been limited to kangaroos, cats, dogs and birds. The idea that someone as young as Molly could die seemed completely wrong and was summed when my young brother asked, "Are ya sure that she isn't just pretending? Us kids do that sometimes ya know."

The matron, no longer the large formidable woman who tended our cuts and scrapes, gently took Edward's hands, "No love, I'm sorry but she is not pretending this time."

"What made her die," I asked.

The matron answered again, "We don't know exactly but we do know it was nobody's fault and was an accident."

"What sorta accident?" the three of asked together.

The adults exchanged looks before the sergeant answered, "The best we can tell she got stuck in a tree with a branch against her throat and choked."

At school on Monday Mr. Golding told the assembly, "You will all know by now that one of our best students died on Saturday. A lot of you were her friends and, like you, I will miss her greatly."

I whispered loudly to Ginger in the next row. "He's a bloody liar - two faced mongrel."

The Head saw me talking and exploded, "Tiley even at this sad moment you have the hide to chat on parade, what have you got to say, boy!"

"If Molly was a good kid like you just said why did ya put her down to grade four? An' she didn't have any friends 'cept for me an' Edward an' Ginger."

Strangely he took my outburst without comment and ordered the assembly to march into class. Later that morning the Sergeant came to the school and talked with a few of the kids. I was the last one to be called into the Head's office for him to speak to. Mr. Golding had been there during the other interviews; however, he asked the Head if Miss. Berry could sit in while he spoke to me. The Head wasn't happy about this turn of events but agreed if that was what the Sergeant wanted.

I wasn't actually questioned. It was more like the officer just wanted to have a yarn about Molly. We talked for about an hour and several times I started to cry because I really felt that if I had stuck up for her more she may not have played the wag and wouldn't have had the accident.

"That's rubbish lad." said the Sergeant. "I have spoken to a lot of the kids today and the one thing they all say is that you were the one that did stick up for the poor girl. One even reckoned that Molly told them you were like her brother."

One question he did ask confused me, and it wasn't until years later that I finally worked out what he was getting at.

"You have told me Molly was sad, John. Do you think she was sad enough just to not care about anything anymore?"

"All she cared about was reading." I replied "An' I reckon when she got put down she was sad, but after the fight with Helen I reckon she got sad like ya said."

Mr. Wodomo asked if Ginger and I would help carry the coffin. He and Dad took one end and we took the other. Mum thought it would look nice if we wore our scout uniforms because Molly once told her how smart she reckoned we looked when we were going to scouts. I was surprised how many people came to the funeral and my Mum said to Dad on the way home from the cemetery, "Bloody hypocrites! Pity they didn't give Molly and Tex the time of the day while she was alive, it might have made all the difference if they had. Also Golding's wife crying in church was probably because she is frightened he will lose his job over this affair." Dad shushed Mum because of us kids but I could see him nodding in agreement.

Mr Wodomo and a couple of his friends from the Council came around to our house for a cup of tea after the funeral and it was here that he told my father that he was leaving as soon as Dad could find someone to replace him.

"No reason to stay in town now I don't have my Molly," he said. Dad wasn't surprised and replied,

"Just do what you have to do, Tex, I can always sort things out."

Then a big surprise did come at school on the Monday after the funeral. Mr. Golding wasn't there and assembly was taken by Miss Berry. After the flag and singing God Save the Queen she announced, "I know it will come as a surprise but Mr. Golding has received an urgent transfer and left on the weekend. His replacement will arrive next week so, until then, I will be looking after the entire school. This means that I will ask all the grade seven and eight children to take turns in helping me with the lower grades."

A few weeks later Ginger and I visited the budgie tree for the first time. I don't know what we expected to find but the only difference was that all the nests were now empty.

We sat in the shade and shared a sandwich the way we always did, but somehow things were different now.

"Molly was a good climber ya know," said Ginger.

"For a sheila she was great." I replied. "Wot do ya reckon happened mate?"

"Dunno. When he's drunk me Dad says she just hung herself in the fork 'cause she was unhappy."

"Naw! Nobody is that unhappy. She was just trying to get through that fork like you, an' slipped 'cause the tree was wet an' she got stuck."

"She is a fair cow this ol' tree, maybe we should chop it down, ya know like a dog gets shot if it bites someone."

"That's a bonzer idea mate. Tomorra we'll bring an axe and knock 'er down."

Something came up the next day and, thankfully, we never did take our anger out on that tree. We did however carve Molly's name deep into its trunk and when I visited the site almost forty years later the word 'MOLLY' was still quite readable.

The town still speculates over her death and for someone with no family in the area, her grave is well tended. Perhaps some of those still living in The Gully feel just a little responsible.

****

The new headmaster was a great bloke an' loved sports so I reckon he decided to use it as a way to help the kids he was in charge of to develop physically as well as in the classroom. I reckon he also believed that this would help us get over Molly's sad passing; so within a month of his arrival he had got together with his counterpart at the Convent, a sister Maria, and between them they organised a town football team to travel with the senior team on its next away game.

A combined State and Convent team had never been contemplated prior to this and great care was taken to ensure that equal numbers from each school were selected. To keep it all fair, the Captain would come from the Convent but the thirteenth man would come from the State with the two reserves from the Convent. The State school grounds were used for training, and the three Convent boarders in the team had to obtain special permission to leave the grounds during the week to attend. *The Postmaster was the coach of the Convent's regular side and was appointed to look after the town team. Things were going well and, one afternoon as the boys were packing up after training, he called John aside, "How's it going young Tiley?" he asked me.*

"Great Mr. Jackson I reckon we got a pretty good team." *I told him.*

"So do I, son." *his coach said,* "But I've got a bit of a problem and I would like to talk to you about it."

My first reaction was, that for some unknown reason, I was going to be dropped from the team. In the time it took for the coach to continue I racked my brain for any incident, in or out of school, that would cause this to happen but my mind was immediately put at rest.

"My problem is that, while the committee decided that the Captain should come from the Convent, with your permission, I want to talk to them to see if they would change their mind and have someone from the State, namely you, as the Captain. I am pretty sure that the convent kids on the team will be happy, so what do you say?"

You could have knocked me down with a feather. One second I was trying to work out why I was being dropped and now I'm being told by the coach that he wants me to be the captain of the team. Once what he had told me had finally sunk in, I told him, "I've never been a captain of anything like this before, an' ol' Father Garvey will be cranky I'll bet ya." *At this Joey Jackson laughed and told me,* "Actually it was the good Father who came to me and suggested that the committee should perhaps change their mind over where the Captain should come from. He reckons you are the best player the Gully has seen for a long time and assures me there will be no problems from the green side of the committee, if I was to make you Captain."

I was more than a little puzzled by what he had said, "What's the green side of the committee?" *I wanted to know. The coach patted me on the shoulder and explained,* "It's just what the Catholic or Convent members are known as, because green is the Irish colour and nearly all Irish are Catholic."

"Oh! My Mum an' Dad call the Irish people Micks. They reckon it's not bad to call 'em that, you know like Ol' Mad Mick but I think that's his real name so he's Mad Mick the Mick, but we have to call him Mister O'Connell".

The coach was keen to know what I thought about the idea of me being the Captain and continued, "I think most of the kids would like you to be the Captain and as we have not actually named anyone from the Convent boys *in the team I don't feel there will be any worries. Of course, I want to talk to your parents but before I do that, it is important you tell me what you reckon."*

Like all the State school kids I had accepted that the Captain would come from the Convent, but we also knew in reality, on the field Baz and I would be leading the team. Something I was very proud of.

Mr. Jackson obviously thought I was good enough to be the Captain but one thing worried me and that was the make up of the team, and asked, *"If I was the Captain would this mean that one of the State school kids would be replaced as the thirteenth bloke in the team, 'cause I don't want that t' happen that's for sure."*

His coach laughed again. *"You've got the makings of a good union man young Tiley. No, you don't have to worry about the make-up of the team: that will remain the same. If the team was picked properly there would be eight state kids and only five from the Convent and your little brother would be the full back. It is all pretty fair but I definitely want you as the Captain. The team you will be playing doesn't have any kids under grade five, so our little blokes will need a good Captain to look after them. So, we go and talk to your Mum and Dad eh?"*

Like me, Mum and Dad were flattered that Joey Jackson thought that I would make a good Captain of the town team, but they were more concerned about any political fallout.

"You don't have to worry about that" they were told. *"You under-estimate the power of the pulpit."*

The town definitely took the team to heart and the announcement of the Captain was accepted without a shrug of dissent. It could even be said that this act of uniting the town under one flag went a long way to determining the team captain's (my) future.

We didn't win the inter town match, but I won the best and fairest prize donated by the sponsor of the senior team. He was the owner of the local garage and a strong Catholic and as it was in those days his policy to employ only family or those belonging to the faith, however in my case he made an exception.

A few years later after a rather unhappy and unsuccessful time at high school I was looking for an apprenticeship and, despite knowing his feelings about non-Catholics, I wrote him an application. To my surprise not only did he remember me but was more than happy to give me a job. I returned to The

Gully for another four fantastic years, in those days an apprenticeship was a very serious matter and, being a minor living away from home I had to have a legal guardian that was what Frank became.

I did meet Mr. Wodomo again in the early eighties; he was working on a drilling rig in Western Australia. I recognised him by that beautiful knife he still carried. We had a meal together and caught up on almost thirty years. Afterwards he asked me back to his donga for a cup of tea, and while I was waiting for it to brew he gave me an old photo album to look at.

*There were a few of the 'plane crash and of course lots of Molly. One in particular caught my eye. This was a photo of Molly, Ginger and myself outside our house. Underneath it, written in scratchy child's printing, was '**Me and me brothers**'.*

Printed in the United States
By Bookmasters